# Fron

# Walt Disney World®
# with Your Family

### *4th Edition*

by Laura Miller

**WILEY**

Wiley Publishing, Inc.

Published by:

# WILEY PUBLISHING, INC.

111 River St.
Hoboken, NJ 07030-5774

ISBN 978-1-118-02756-1

Editor: Jessica Langan-Peck
Production Editor: Heather Wilcox
Cartographer: Guy Ruggiero
Photo Editor: Richard Fox
Production by Wiley Indianapolis Composition Services

Front cover photo: Kids at Epcot © Gary Bogdon Photography
Back cover photo: Disney characters at Magic Kingdom © Gary Bogdon Photography

For information on our other products and services or to obtain technical support,
please contact our Customer Care Department within the U.S. at 800/762-2974, outside the U.S. at 317/572-3993 or fax 317/572-4002.

Wiley also publishes its books in a variety of electronic formats. Some content that
appears in print may not be available in electronic formats.

Manufactured in the United States of America

5  4  3  2  1

# CONTENTS

## 3 GETTING TO KNOW WALT DISNEY WORLD · 33

## 4 WHERE TO STAY · 43

## 5 WHERE TO DINE · 72

## 6 EXPLORING WALT DISNEY WORLD  100

# LIST OF MAPS

## ABOUT THE AUTHOR

**Laura Miller** is a freelance writer who divides her time between Orchard Park, New York, and the Florida coast. She's spent countless hours scouring through Central Florida's various theme parks, hotels, resorts, and restaurants over the years (too many to count)—both with and without her five children. A family-travel expert who religiously travels to the Land the Mouse Built several times throughout the year, she also operates **travel-insights.com**, a website dedicated to Central Florida and the art of family travel.

## HOW TO CONTACT US

In researching this book, we discovered many wonderful places—hotels, restaurants, shops, and more. We're sure you'll find others. Please tell us about them, so we can share the information with your fellow travelers in upcoming editions. If you were disappointed with a recommendation, we'd love to know that, too. Please write to:

*Frommer's Walt Disney World with Your Family,* 4th Edition
Wiley Publishing, Inc. • 111 River St. • Hoboken, NJ 07030-5774

## AN ADDITIONAL NOTE

Please be advised that travel information is subject to change at any time—and this is especially true of prices. We therefore suggest that you write or call ahead for confirmation when making your travel plans. The authors, editors, and publisher cannot be held responsible for the experiences of readers while traveling. Your safety is important to us, however, so we encourage you to stay alert and be aware of your surroundings. Keep a close eye on cameras, purses, and wallets, all favorite targets of thieves and pickpockets.

# FROMMER'S STAR RATINGS, ICONS & ABBREVIATIONS

Every hotel, restaurant, and attraction listing in this guide has been ranked for quality, value, service, amenities, and special features using a **star-rating system.** In country, state, and regional guides, we also rate towns and regions to help you narrow down your choices and budget your time accordingly. Hotels and restaurants are rated on a scale of zero (recommended) to three stars (exceptional). Attractions, shopping, nightlife, towns, and regions are rated according to the following scale: zero stars (recommended), one star (highly recommended), two stars (very highly recommended), and three stars (must-see).

In addition to the star-rating system, we also use **seven feature icons** that point you to the great deals, in-the-know advice, and unique experiences that separate travelers from tourists. Throughout the book, look for:

| | |
|---|---|
| **Finds** | Special finds—those places only insiders know about |
| **Fun Facts** | Fun facts—details that make travelers more informed and their trips more fun |
| **Kids** | Best bets for kids and advice for the whole family |
| **Moments** | Special moments—those experiences that memories are made of |
| **Overrated** | Places or experiences not worth your time or money |
| **Tips** | Insider tips—great ways to save time and money |
| **Value** | Great values—where to get the best deals |

The following **abbreviations** are used for credit cards:

| | | | | | |
|---|---|---|---|---|---|
| **AE** | American Express | **DISC** | Discover | **V** | Visa |
| **DC** | Diners Club | **MC** | MasterCard | | |

## TRAVEL RESOURCES AT FROMMERS.COM

Frommer's travel resources don't end with this guide. Frommer's website, **www.frommers.com**, has travel information on more than 4,000 destinations. We update features regularly, giving you access to the most current trip-planning information and the best airfare, lodging, and car-rental bargains. You can also listen to podcasts, connect with other Frommers.com members through our active-reader forums, share your travel photos, read blogs from guidebook editors and fellow travelers, and much more.

# The Best of Walt Disney World & Orlando

**In the beginning, Orlando may have been a sleepy** little southern town filled with farmland as far as the eye could see, orange groves galore, and only two attractions to its name (a water-ski show and some great big gators). Then came the Mouse. More specifically, a mouse named Mickey and his creator, a man of fantastic imagination and vision named Walt Disney. Life in Orlando would never be the same. Since the opening of Walt Disney World back in 1971, Orlando has grown to become one of the world's top vacation destinations. Almost 49 million people from all parts of the world make their way to this city each year to sample its unending array of exciting, unique, and diverse activities. Those of us who continue to return year after year can count on each new visit to provide a host of new experiences and memories.

When Disney World first opened its gates to the public, I doubt if anyone but Walt Disney, the original Imagineer, could have predicted what lay ahead. Disney's legacy, while commercialized over the years, has practically become a rite of passage, not to mention a national shrine to which visitors flock by the millions. The opening of Walt Disney World's Magic Kingdom started a tourist boom in Central Florida the likes of which has never been seen elsewhere. Today, The Kingdom That Walt Built entices visitors with four theme parks, a dozen smaller attractions, two nightclub districts, tens of thousands of hotel rooms, a vacation club (otherwise known as timeshares), scores of restaurants, and even three cruise ships (soon to be four). All in all, there are more than 100 attractions, Disney and not, large and small, that will keep you

> **(Fun Facts)** **By the Numbers**
>
> Orlando's theme parks, though seeing increasing atten-
> dance levels, are still affected by the recent downturn
> in the economy. Though predictions state that levels will
> continue to rise over the next few years, they will likely
> do so at a much slower pace. Parks however continue
> to entice visitors to return and to stay longer by offering
> special deals and discounts and by adding wild and
> wonderfully new attractions. Here are the 2009 atten-
> dance estimates (and their national rankings) for all of
> the major Orlando parks according to TEA Inc. and
> Economic Research Associates:
>
> - No. 1: Magic Kingdom, 17.2 million (+1%)
> - No. 3: Epcot, 11 million (+8%)
> - No. 4: Disney's Hollywood Studios, 9.7 million (+1%)
> - No. 5: Disney's Animal Kingdom, 9.6 million (+.5%)

coming back for more. There are also plenty of restaurants, ranging
from fine dining to on-the-fly fast food; many of the more casual
restaurants are as themed as the parks themselves. And the city
doesn't lack for hotels and resorts either, with more than 116,000
rooms, villas, and suites to go around (and even more on the way).
If you can believe it, the landscape is still changing, evolving, growing, and expanding to ensure your experiences will do the same
each and every time you stay and play in Orlando.

## 1 THE BEST ORLANDO EXPERIENCES

- **Explore Disney's Animal Kingdom:** Explore Disney's most
  spectacular and wildest Imagineering to date. Trek through the
  jungles of Africa along the Pangani Forest Exploration Trail or

set out on safari across the savanna with Kilimanjaro Safaris. Journey through the exotic lands of Asia and embark on an expedition to the peaks of Expedition Everest; then explore the mysteries of Anandapur wandering the Maharajah Jungle Trek. Be sure not to miss *Finding Nemo—The Musical* or *The Festival of the Lion King,* absolutely the best shows in all of WDW. See p. 170.

- **Go Globe-Trotting at Epcot:** You can travel around the world in only an afternoon at the World Showcase pavilions, rocket through space on a thrilling mission to Mars at Mission: Space, travel back in time to the age of the dinosaurs at the Universe of Energy, and dive deep below the sea to explore the ocean's inhabitants at The Seas with Nemo & Friends. And there's no better way to cap your day off than watching Epcot's IllumiNations, a spectacular fireworks, laser lights, and fountain show. See p. 137.

- **Take Center Stage at Disney's Hollywood Studios:** Though it is more grown-up than the Magic Kingdom, it has plenty of great shows to entertain the kids and attractions to thrill movie buffs. Don't miss Toy Story Mania, Twilight Zone Tower of Terror, Rock 'n' Roller Coaster, and Fantasmic!—an innovative, after-dark mix of live action, waterworks, fireworks, and laser lights that rivals IllumiNations. See p. 158.

- **Escape to the Magic Kingdom:** It may seem an obvious choice, but Disney's oldest is still the most magical of Orlando's theme parks. Speed through the universe on Space Mountain, watch Donald's antics at Mickey's PhilharMagic, laugh out loud at the Monsters, Inc. Laugh Floor, or wave hello to the ghouls of the Haunted Mansion. Cap your day with the impressive Wishes fireworks display. There's plenty here to entertain all ages. See p. 109.

## 2  THE BEST THRILL RIDES

Orlando lays claim to some of the biggest and baddest thrill rides and roller coasters anywhere—certainly one of the largest collections of them in any one locale. So if your idea of fun is to twist and turn at speeds only a jet should reach, dive uncontrollably from dizzying heights to below ground level and back, or see just

## Orlando's Best Websites

Considering that Orlando welcomes more than 48 million visitors each year, it should come as no surprise that literally hundreds of websites are devoted to vacationing here. These include information on just about everything, from the history of Walt Disney World to getting around town.

There are several sites written by Disney fans, employees, and self-proclaimed experts. A favorite (www.hidden mickeys.org) is all about **Hidden Mickeys,** a park tradition (see chapter 6, "Exploring Walt Disney World"). These subtle Disney images can be found scattered throughout the realm, though they sometimes are in the eye, or imagination, of the beholder. **Deb's Unofficial Walt Disney World Information Guide** (www.allearsnet.com) is the best around, loaded with great tips and information on everything Disney from the parks and resorts to the restaurants, nightlife, and much more. It now includes information on Universal Orlando as well.

Definitely take a look at Disney's official site, **www. disneyworld.com**, which was recently overhauled, if you're planning a pilgrimage to the House of Mouse. It's loaded

how far up into your throat your stomach can go—this is the place for you. Here are the city's top stomach churners and G-force generators.

- **Rock 'n' Roller Coaster** (Disney's Hollywood Studios): You'll launch from 0 to 60 mph in 2.8 seconds, heading straight into the first of several inversions as 120 speakers in your "stretch limo" blast Aerosmith at (yeeeow!) 32,000 watts right into your ears. To add to the thrill of this indoor coaster, the entire experience takes place in the dark. See p. 166.

with some excellent photos and 360-degree views of Disney's resorts, rooms, parks, and more. **Magical Gatherings,** available on the Disney site as well, is a free downloadable online tool allowing you to plan your group's Disney vacation. You can plan itineraries, take group polls, list everyone's favorites, and even chat to come up with the perfect plan. **My Disney Vacation,** also available on the Disney site, allows you to plan your entire Disney vacation from start to finish—you can create your very own customized theme park maps to mirror the itinerary you've planned out online.

If you're looking to save a few dollars, try **Mousesavers** (www.mousesavers.com), which features information, insider Disney tips, and (the biggest perk) exclusive discounted deals for area hotels, resorts, and packages.

Though a relative newcomer, **Travel Insights Online** (www.travel-insights.com) is filled with travel tips, indepth reviews, and information on Disney, including reviews of the area's kid-friendliest restaurants and resorts.

- **Summit Plummet** (Disney's Blizzard Beach): This one starts slow, with a lift ride (even in Florida's 100°F/38°C dog days) to the 120-foot summit. But it finishes with the (self-proclaimed) world's fastest body slide—a test of your courage and swimsuit—as it virtually goes straight down and has you moving sans vehicle at 60 mph by the end. See p. 186.
- **Twilight Zone Tower of Terror** (Disney's Hollywood Studios): The name says it all. The ride transports guests into the Twilight Zone as a haunted hotel's service elevator slowly rises—only to

plummet 13 stories, terrifying those inside. But the freefall fun doesn't end there. The tower's computer program randomly alternates drop sequences to make sure you never experience the same ride twice. When you get off and your legs finally stop shaking, *some of you* will want to ride again. See p. 168.

## 3 THE BEST MODERATELY PRICED ACCOMMODATIONS

- **Disney's Port Orleans Resort** (Lake Buena Vista; ℂ **407/934-7639** or 407/934-5000): Here's a good value by Disney standards. It has dual Southern charm in its French Quarter and Riverside areas, and the pool has a water slide curving from the mouth of a colorful dragon. See p. 55.
- **Hilton in the Walt Disney World Resort** (Lake Buena Vista; ℂ **407/827-4000**): It's the only official resort on Hotel Plaza Boulevard to offer Disney's Extra Magic Hour option. Other pluses include a huge variety of services, two pools, and spacious junior suites. And it has a great location next to Downtown Disney. See p. 63.
- **Lake Buena Vista Resort Village & Spa** (Lake Buena Vista; ℂ **866/401-2699** or 407/597-0214): Off the beaten path, yet close to Disney, this upscale resort's oversized two-, three-, and four-bedroom suites have full kitchens, washers and dryers, and plasma TVs. A 7,300-square-foot pirate-themed pool will keep the kids entertained, while the full-service spa ensures the adults will remain relaxed. See p. 68.
- **Staybridge Suites Lake Buena Vista** (Lake Buena Vista; ℂ **800/866-4549** or 407/238-0777): Close to the action of Downtown Disney and the theme parks, this resort's one- and two-bedroom suites have full kitchens and are larger and more comfortable than most of the competition. And breakfast is on the resort—a complimentary buffet of hot and cold items is set out daily so you don't have to deal with the hassle of dining elsewhere. See p. 70.

# 4 THE BEST THEME RESTAURANTS

Orlando has elevated themed dining to an art form. The food at these restaurants may not be the best in town (though it won't be terrible either), but you can't beat the atmosphere.

- **World Showcase restaurants** (Epcot; ℭ **407/939-3463**): Epcot's World Showcase is home to Orlando's best collection of theme restaurants in one setting. Dine in next to a gigantic aquarium, chow down in Germany, or watch a belly dancer do her thing as you eat couscous in Morocco. You'll have a blast no matter which dining spot you choose. See p. 82.

- **Sci-Fi Dine-In Theater Restaurant** (Disney's Hollywood Studios; ℭ **407/939-3463**): Your table is set inside a 1950s-era convertible, your carhop (umm . . . waitress) serves you popcorn as an appetizer, and you can zone out on sci-fi flicks on a giant movie screen while you eat. It's an out-of-this-world experience. See p. 84.

- **T-Rex Café** (Downtown Disney Marketplace; ℭ **407/828-8739**): Set some million or so years in the past, this paleontologist's playground is waiting to be explored—especially if you're dining with the kids. Bubbling geysers, a fossil dig site, life-sized animatronic dinosaurs, an hourly meteorite shower, eerily glowing rooms, and themes of fire and ice—it's all here. It's definitely one of the most creative dining spots at Disney.

- **50's Prime Time Café** (Disney's Hollywood Studios; ℭ **407/939-3463**): Ozzie and Harriet would feel right at home inside this replica of Mom's kitchen (ca. 1950), where classic TV shows play on black-and-white screens. Servers may threaten to withhold dessert (choices include s'mores!) if you don't finish your meatloaf, so clean that plate! See p. 81.

# 2

# Planning Your Trip to Walt Disney World

Winging it once you get there simply won't do when your destination is Walt Disney World. Without some pretrip preparation, you'll likely find yourself so overwhelmed upon arriving in Orlando that you'll miss out on exactly what it was you came for in the first place—fun. In this chapter, you'll find just about everything you need to know before you go, including tons of helpful information to get you started.

## 1 WHEN TO GO

Orlando is the theme-park capital of the world, and you could almost argue that there really is no off-season here, though the busiest seasons are whenever kids are out of school. Late May to just past Labor Day, long holiday weekends, winter holidays (mid-Dec to early Jan), and most especially spring break (late Mar to Apr) are very busy. Do, however, keep in mind that kids in other hemispheres follow a completely different schedule altogether.

Peak-season rates can go into effect during large conventions and special events, either of which may occur at any time of the year. Even something as remote as Bike Week in Daytona Beach (about an hour by car northeast) can raise prices. These kinds of events will especially impact the moderately priced hotels and resorts located off Walt Disney World.

**Best times:** The week after Labor Day until the week before Thanksgiving when the kids have just returned to school; the week

**Tips** **Weather Wise**

It's not uncommon for the skies to open up on Orlando, even when the day begins with the sun ablaze. Florida is well known for its afternoon downpours, so don't be too concerned—storms don't usually last too long It is wise, however, to bring along some type of rain gear as storms can spring up rather quickly. Rain ponchos can be purchased throughout the parks for about $6 for a child-size poncho, or $8 for an adult size.

Don't let a rainy afternoon spoil your fun. Crowds are dramatically thinner on these days and there are plenty of indoor attractions to enjoy, particularly at Epcot and Disney's Hollywood Studios. The flip side, of course, is that many of the outdoor rides and attractions are temporarily closed during downpours and lightning storms.

after Thanksgiving until mid-December, and the 6 weeks before and after school spring vacations (which generally occur around Easter).

*Worst times:* The absolute worst time of year to visit is during spring break—usually the 2 weeks prior to and after Easter. The crowds are unbelievable, the lines are unbearable (my kids have waited upwards of 2 hr. to hop on some of the most popular attractions), waiting times at local restaurants can lead to starvation, and traffic—particularly on International Drive—will give you a headache. The December holidays and summer, when out-of-state visitors take advantage of school breaks and many locals bring their families to the parks (the latter also flock to the parks during Florida resident discount months, which usually fall in May and Nov) can also prove a challenge. Packed parking lots are the norm during the week before and after Christmas, and the summer brings with it oppressive heat and humidity.

*Seriously consider pulling your kids out of school* for a few days around an off-season weekend to avoid the long lines. Even during these periods, though, the number of international visitors guarantees you won't be alone.

One other time-related hazard: For several weeks in May and September you will find yourself in the midst of the dreaded "love bug" season in Central Florida. These small flylike insects emerge twice a year, get into practically everything, and like nothing more than to commit suicide on your car windshield, leaving a messy splatter. They don't bite, but are a serious nuisance. If you can avoid them, I highly recommend it.

Hurricane season generally runs from around June 1 to November 30 (when the majority of Central Florida's afternoon downpours tend to occur). Inland, the worst is usually only sheets of rain and enough wind to wipe the smile right off your face. That said, the summer of 2004 (when three hurricanes passed through the area) was a noticeable reminder that the worst can happen, and 2005 brought with it what seemed like an endless number of storms, extending the rainy season well beyond the normal timeline. And while 2006 was relatively quiet weather-wise, tornados touched down and devastated areas just north of Orlando in 2007. The moral of this story—be prepared, because almost anything can happen. Forecasters predict an increased number of storms in 2011, but how many will actually reach land (or affect areas as far inland as Orlando) is unknown.

# ORLANDO AREA CALENDAR OF EVENTS

For an exhaustive list of events beyond those listed here, check **http://events.frommers.com**, where you'll find a searchable, up-to-the-minute roster of what's happening in not only Orlando, but in cities all over the world.

**JANUARY**

**Walt Disney World Marathon.** About 90% of the 16,000 runners finish this 26.2-mile "sprint" through the resort area and parks ($135). It's open to anyone 18 and older, including runners with disabilities as long as they are able to maintain the 16-minute mile-pacing requirements. There's also a half-marathon ($135), Goofy's Race-and-a-Half Challenge (includes registration for both marathons; $310), a Family Fun Run 5K for kids and adults ($45), and Mickey's Marathon Kid Fest that includes the Mickey Mile ($25 per child) and a handful of shorter races for the 13-and-under set—including a diaper dash ($10 per child). Call ℂ **407/939-7810,** or go to **www.disney sports.com** for information on participating. January 6 to 9.

### FEBRUARY

**Atlanta Braves.** The Braves have been holding spring training at Disney's Wide World of Sports Complex since 1998. There are 15 home games during the 1-month season. (The team arrives in mid-Feb; games begin in early Mar.) Tickets are $15 to $39. You can get more information at ℂ **407/939-GAME (4236)** or **www.disneysports.com**. To purchase tickets, call Ticketmaster at ℂ **877/803-7073** or 407/839-3900. You can also get online information at **www.atlantabraves.com** or **www.majorleague baseball.com**.

### APRIL

**Epcot International Flower and Garden Festival.** This 6-weeks-long event showcases gardens, topiary characters, floral displays, speakers, seminars, and nightly entertainment. The festival is free with regular park admission ($82 adults, $74 kids 3–9). For more information, call ℂ **407/934-7639** or visit **www.disneyworld.com**. The festival kicks off in late April and goes through early June.

### MAY

**Star Wars Weekends.** Every year, Disney features a fan-fest full of activities for *Star Wars* fanatics. Characters are on hand for up-close meet-and-greets, as well as a handful of *Star Wars* actors. Games, parades, and special entertainment top off the festivities. The celebrations run for 5 consecutive weekends beginning in May and are included in park admission ($82 adult, $74 kids 3–9).

**Gay Days.** The first weekend in June attracts tens of thousands of gays and lesbians to Central Florida for what amounts, with add-ons, to a week of festivities. It grew out of "Gay Day," held unofficially at Disney World since the early 1990s and drawing some 100,000 people to the area. Look for online information on discounts, packages, hosts, and more at **www.gaydays.com**. Also, see "For Gay & Lesbian Families," later in this chapter.

### JULY

**Independence Day.** Disney adds a bit of sparkle to their fireworks displays at all the Disney parks, which stay open later than normal. Call 🕐 **407/934-7639** for details or surf over to **www.disneyworld.com**.

### SEPTEMBER

**Night of Joy.** The first weekend (Thurs–Sun) in September, the Magic Kingdom hosts a festival of contemporary Christian music featuring top artists. This is a very popular event, so obtain tickets early. Performers also make an appearance at Long's Christian Bookstore in College Park, about 20 minutes north of Disney. Admission (if you buy in advance) to the concert is $49.95 for 1 night (7:30pm–12:30am), $89.95 for 2 nights; single-night admission at the gate is $57.95. Use of Magic Kingdom attractions is included. Call 🕐 **407/934-7639** for concert details; for information about the free appearance at Long's, call 🕐 **407/422-6934.**

### OCTOBER

**Mickey's Not-So-Scary Halloween Party.** The Magic Kingdom (🕐 **407/934-7639;** www.disneyworld.com) invites you to join Mickey and his pals for a far-from-frightening time. Come in costume and trick-or-treat throughout the Magic Kingdom from 7pm to midnight on any of 10 or so nights. The alcohol-free party includes parades, live music, and storytelling. The climax is a bewitching fireworks spectacular. A separate admission fee is charged ($53.95–$59.95 adults, $47.95–$53.95 kids 3–9; depending on the night), and you should get tickets well in advance.

**Epcot International Food & Wine Festival.** Here's your chance to sip and savor the food and beverages of more than 20 cultures. Events include wine tastings for adults, seminars, food, dinners, concerts, and celebrity-chef cooking demonstrations. Tickets for the dinner-and-concert series or wine tastings run approximately $35 to $130, including gratuity; signature dinners and vertical wine tastings range from $100 to $375 (sometimes more). The event also features 25 food-and-wine marketplaces where appetizer-size portions of dishes ranging from pizza to escargot (and everything in between) sell for less than $7 each. Entrance to the festival is included in park admission. Call ✆ **407/934-7639** for details or check out **www.disneyworld.com**. Early October to mid-November.

NOVEMBER

**The Osborne Family Spectacle of Lights.** This classic holiday attraction returned by popular demand after being closed down for renovations in 2004 and 2005. Lighting up the nights at the Disney's Hollywood Studios are millions of sparkling bulbs acquired from a family whose Christmas light collection got a bit too bright for their neighbors. The holiday display runs from November to early January.

DECEMBER

**Christmas at Walt Disney World.** During the holiday festivities, Main Street in the Magic Kingdom is lavishly decked out with twinkling lights and Christmas holly, all the while carolers are greeting visitors throughout the park. Epcot, Disney's Hollywood Studios, and Animal Kingdom also offer special embellishments and entertainment throughout the holiday season, and the Disney resorts are decked out with towering Christmas trees, wreaths, boughs, and bows.

Some holiday highlights include **Mickey's Very Merry Christmas Party,** an after-dark (7pm–midnight) ticketed event ($53.95–$59.95 adults, $47.95–$53.95 kids 3–9). This takes place on select nights at the Magic Kingdom and offers a festive parade, fireworks, special shows, and admission to a handful of rides. Also included are cookies, cocoa, and a souvenir photo.

> (Fun Facts) **Disney in December**
>
> No snow? No problem. Although there may be a lack of the white stuff in Orlando during the month of December (or any other month for that matter), WDW more than makes up for it by decking the halls as only Disney can: 11 miles of garlands, 3,000 wreaths, and 1,500 Christmas trees decorate Walt Disney World during the holiday season.

**Holidays Around the World** and the **Candlelight Procession** at Epcot feature hundreds of carolers, storytellers from a host of international countries, celebrity narrators telling the Christmas story, a 450-voice choir, and a 50-piece orchestra in a very moving display. Fireworks are included. Regular admission ($82 adults, $74 kids 3–9) is required. Call ✆ **407/934-7639** for details on all of the above, or go to **www.disneyworld.com**. The holiday fun lasts from mid-December to early January.

**Walt Disney World New Year's Eve Celebration.** For 1 night a year, the Magic Kingdom stays open until the wee hours for a massive fireworks explosion. Other New Year's festivities in WDW include a special Hoop-Dee-Doo Musical Revue at Fort Wilderness, and guest performances by well-known musical groups at Disney's Hollywood Studios and Epcot. Call ✆ **407/934-7639** for details, or visit **www.disneyworld.com**. December 31.

## 2 GETTING THERE

### BY PLANE

More than 50 scheduled airlines and several more charter companies serve the more than 34 million passengers who land in

Orlando each year. **Southwest** (℅ **800/435-9792;** www.southwest. com) has once again recaptured the top spot, claiming more than 22% of the flights in and out of the **Orlando International Airport** (MCO). Second place goes to **AirTran Airways** (℅ **800/247-8726;** www.airtran.com), at just over 12.7%, while **Delta** (℅ **800/221-1212;** www.delta.com) and **JetBlue** (℅ **800/538-2583;** www. jetblue.com) tie for third, each with slightly more than 11% of the flights.

## Orlando's Airports

**Orlando International Airport** (℅ **407/825-2001;** www.state. fl.us/goaa) offers direct or nonstop service from 73 U.S. cities and two dozen international destinations. **All major car-rental companies** are located at or near the airport.

   **Orlando Sanford International Airport** (SFB; ℅ **407/585-4000;** www.orlandosanfordairport.com) is much smaller than the main airport, but it has grown a bit in recent years, thanks mainly to a small fleet of international carriers. The airport has **Avis, Alamo, Budget, Dollar, Enterprise, Hertz, National, and Thrifty** rental-car desks on-site. It is also served by Mears Transportation shuttles (see below).

## Getting into Town from the Airport

Orlando International is 25 miles east of Walt Disney World and 20 miles south of downtown. At rush hour (7–9am and 4–6pm), the drive can be torture and take up to an hour or more; at other times, it's about 30 to 40 minutes depending on your exact destination. **Mears Transportation Group** (℅ **407/423-5566;** www. mearstransportation.com) has vans that shuttle passengers from the airport (you catch them at ground level) to the Disney resorts and official hotels, as well as most other Orlando properties. Their air-conditioned vehicles operate round-the-clock, departing every 15 to 25 minutes in either direction. Rates vary by destination. Round-trip fares for adults run $29 ($23 for kids 4–11) between the airport and International Drive; $45 ($36 for kids 4–11) for Walt Disney World/Lake Buena Vista or West U.S. 192. Children 3 and younger ride free.

**Quicksilver Tours and Transportation** (✆ **888/468-6939** or 407/299-1434; www.quicksilver-tours.com) is a bit more personal. Their folks greet you at baggage claim with a sign bearing your name—they'll even help with your luggage. The bonus is a 30-minute grocery stop and free phone call included in the price. While a bit more expensive than Mears, they're coming for you. And they're only going to *your* resort. This is a good option for four or more people. Rates run from $125 (up to 10 people, round-trip) to I-Drive, $130 to Universal Studios, and $130 to $135 for the Disney empire.

**Tiffany Towncar** (✆ **888/838-2161** or 407/370-2196; www. tiffanytowncar.com) offers a $125 round-trip rate for up to seven people, $135 for eight to 10 from Orlando International to I-Drive, Universal, Disney, and U.S. 192. Drivers will meet you right at baggage claim, and a free 30-minute grocery stop is included with the service. Booster and car seats are available upon request (at no charge).

To drive yourself from the airport to the attractions, take the **North** exit out of the airport to **Highway 528 West.** Follow signs to **I-4;** it takes about 30 to 40 minutes to get to Walt Disney World if the traffic isn't too heavy (however, you can double that if it is rush hour or if there's an accident). When you get to I-4, follow the signs **west** toward the attractions. Most Orlando car-rental agencies will provide you with maps that will show how to get to your hotel; be sure and ask for one at the rental counter.

## BY CAR

Orlando is 436 miles from Atlanta; 1,312 miles from Boston; 1,120 miles from Chicago; 1,009 miles from Cleveland; 1,170 miles from Dallas; 1,114 miles from Detroit; and 1,088 miles from New York City.

- From Atlanta, take I-75 south to the Florida Turnpike to I-4 west.
- From points northeast, take I-95 south to Daytona Beach and I-4 west.

- From Chicago, take I-65 south to Nashville, then I-24 south to I-75, and then south on the Florida Turnpike to I-4 west.
- From Cleveland, take I-77 south to Columbia, S.C., and then I-26 east to I-95 south to I-4 west.
- From Dallas, take I-20 east to I-49, south to I-10, east to I-75, and then south on the Florida Turnpike to I-4 west.
- From Detroit, take I-75 south to the Florida Turnpike, and then exit on I-4 west.

## BY TRAIN

**Amtrak** trains (© **800/872-7245;** www.amtrak.com) pull into stations at 1400 Sligh Blvd. in downtown Orlando (23 miles from Walt Disney World), and 111 Dakin Ave. in Kissimmee (15 miles from WDW). There are also stops in Winter Park, 10 miles north of downtown Orlando, at 150 W. Morse Blvd.; and in Sanford, 23 miles northeast of downtown Orlando, 800 Persimmon Ave.

**FARES**    As with airline fares, you can occasionally get discounts if you book far in advance. There may be some restrictions on travel dates for discounted fares, mostly around very busy holiday times. Amtrak also offers money-saving packages—including accommodations (some at WDW resorts), car rentals, tours, and train fare (© **800/872-7245**).

## 3   MONEY & COSTS

**ATMs** are located on Main Street in the Magic Kingdom and at the entrances to Epcot, Disney's Hollywood Studios, and Animal Kingdom (where you'll find another one located across from the TriceraTop Spin in DinoLand).

Outside the parks, most malls have at least one ATM, and they're in some convenience stores, such as 7-Elevens and Circle Ks, as well as in grocery stores and drugstores.

*Note:* Many banks impose a fee every time you use a card at another bank's ATM, and the bank from which you withdraw cash may charge its own fee. To compare banks' ATM fees within the U.S., use **www.bankrate.com**.

You can also buy **Disney dollars** (currency with the images of Mickey, Minnie, Pirates of the Caribbean, and so on) in $1, $5, and $10 denominations. They're good at WDW shops, restaurants, and resorts, as well as Disney stores everywhere. If you have any dollar leftovers, you can exchange them for real currency upon leaving WDW, or keep them as a souvenir. *Note:* Pay close attention if you have a refund coming. Some items, such as strollers, wheelchairs, and lockers, require a deposit, and Disney staffers will frequently use Mickey money for refunds instead of the cash. If you don't want it, just let them know and they'll be happy to give you real cash.

## CREDIT CARDS & DEBIT CARDS

It's highly recommended that you travel with at least one major credit card or your debit card. You must have a credit card to rent a car, and hotels and airlines usually require a credit card imprint as a deposit against expenses.

Disney parks, resorts, shops, and restaurants (but not most fast-food outlets) accept five major credit cards: **American Express, Diners Club, Discover, MasterCard,** and **Visa.** Additionally, the WDW resorts will let you charge purchases made in their respective park shops and restaurants to your hotel room, but you must settle up when you check out. Be sure, however, to keep track of your spending as you go along so you won't be surprised when you get the total bill.

# 4 HEALTH

## COMMON AILMENTS

Limit your exposure to Florida's strong sun, especially during the first few days of your trip and, thereafter, during the hours of 11am to 2pm, when the sun is at its strongest. Use a sunscreen with the highest sun protection factor (SPF) available (especially for children) and apply it liberally. If you have children less than a year old, check with your pediatrician before applying a sunscreen—some ingredients may not be appropriate for infants.

## WHAT TO DO IF YOU GET SICK AWAY FROM HOME

Always carry a list of phone numbers that includes your hometown physician, your hometown pharmacy, and your insurance provider, as all will likely be necessary if you find yourself in need of medical attention while away from home. See chapter 7, "Fast Facts," p. 189, for information on finding medical providers in Orlando.

If you suffer from a chronic illness (or even if you're just under the weather prior to your departure), consult your doctor before your departure. Always pack **prescription medications** in your carry-on luggage (so they are readily available even if your checked luggage isn't), and carry them in their original containers, with pharmacy labels—otherwise they won't make it through airport security.

---

# 5 SAFETY

---

Just because Minnie, Mickey, Donald, and Goofy all live here doesn't mean that a few more seedy characters aren't lurking about as well. Even in the most magical place on earth you shouldn't let your guard down; Orlando has a crime rate that's comparable to that of other large U.S. cities. Stay alert and remain aware of your surroundings. It's best to keep your valuables in a safe. Most hotels are equipped with in-room safes or offer the use of a safety deposit box at the front desk, just for that purpose. Keep a close eye on your valuables when you're in public places—restaurants, theaters, and even airport terminals. Renting a locker at the theme parks is always preferable to leaving your valuables in the trunk of your car. Be cautious, even when in the parks, and avoid carrying large amounts of cash in a backpack or fanny pack, which could be easily accessed while you're standing in line for a ride or show. And don't leave valuables unattended under a stroller—that's pretty much asking for them to be stolen.

If you're renting a car while in Orlando, carefully read the safety instructions that the rental company provides. Never stop for any reason in a suspicious, poorly lit, or unpopulated area, and remember that children should never ride in the front seat of a car equipped with air bags.

## KEEPING KIDS SAFE

There is one major safety issue when traveling with kids that usually comes up a lot more frequently in Orlando than it does in other destinations (though it's fortunately not common): the Lost Child.

If a child turns up missing, report it immediately to the closest park employee. After making your report, find out where lost children are brought (there are usually one or two central locations in each park) and head directly there. Odds are your little wanderers are either already there or will arrive shortly.

The best way to prevent any of this from happening is to take a few cautionary steps:

- **Dress young kids in easily identifiable clothing** so you don't lose them in a crowd.
- **Always set up a meeting spot** for your kids to head to, should you all get separated. Pick a place that's central, specific, and easily located (saying "I'll meet you at Cinderella Castle" rather than "I'll meet you at the entrance to Cinderella's Royal Table" is a recipe for disaster).
- **Hold on tight to young kids** (even carry them or secure them in the stroller if possible) when exiting the park at closing time, at parades, and when leaving shows. It's very easy to get separated when you're smack in the middle of a massive wave of people.
- **Sew or affix a name-tag to your child's clothing** (though not in a place it can be read casually) with your child's first name, your cellphone number, and a contact number at home. The minute you get into the park, show your kids the distinctive name-tags that the theme-park employees wear, and tell them to report to one of them if they get lost.

- **Don't assume that rides or restrooms have a single exit.** Always give a specific place for your child to meet you. Otherwise, you may end up in two different spots . . . and at least one of you will panic.

---

## 6 WALT DISNEY WORLD WITH YOUR FAMILY

---

No city in the world is geared more toward family travel than Orlando. Keep an eye out for coupons discounting meals and attractions; they can be found practically everywhere. The Calendar section in Friday's *Orlando Sentinel* newspaper often contains coupons and good deals. Many restaurants, especially those in tourist areas, offer great discounts that are yours for the clipping. Check the information you receive from the Orlando/Orange County Convention & Visitors Bureau (see "Visitor Information," earlier in this chapter), including free or cheap things to do. Additionally, many hotel lobbies and attractions have free coupon books for the taking.

Here are a few suggestions for making traveling with children easier.

- **Are Your Kids Old Enough?** Do you really want to bring an infant or toddler to the parks? If you plan on visiting Disney several times as your children grow, then the best age for a first visit to Disney is just about 3 years old. Why? Because the kids are old enough to walk around, enjoy the sights and sounds, and a good deal of the rides and shows as well. The thrill rides would most likely frighten them, but most inappropriate rides for the tiny tot set have height restrictions that prevent any unfortunate mistakes. If, however, this trip is going to be a one-time trip, then I recommend waiting until your children are between 7 and 10. They'll still be able to appreciate the wonder of the experience but won't have reached the stage where all they'll want is chills and thrills.

• **Planning Ahead**   Make reservations for "character breakfasts" at Disney (see chapter 5, "Where to Dine") as soon as possible. Disney usually accepts them up to 180 days in advance, and many are booked minutes (I'm not kidding!) after the 180-day window opens, so mark your calendar to call (and be sure you keep in mind that the line opens for calls at 7am EST). Also, in any park, check the daily schedule for character appearances (all of the major ones post them on maps or boards near the entrances).

• **Packing**   Although your home may be toddler-proof, hotel accommodations aren't. Bring blank plugs to cover outlets and whatever else is necessary to prevent an accident from occurring in your room. Most hotels have some type of cribs available; however they are usually limited in number.

Outside of hotel supplies, your biggest packing priority should be sunscreen. *Don't forget to bring and use sunscreen with an SPF rating of at least 30.* If you do forget it, it's available at convenience stores, drugstores, and some theme-park shops. Young children should be slathered, even if they're in a stroller, and be sure to pack a wide-brim hat for infants and toddlers. Adults and children alike should drink plenty of water to avoid dehydration.

• **Read the Signs**   Most rides post signs that explain **height restrictions,** if any, or identify those that may unsettle youngsters. Save yourself and your kids some grief before you get in line and are disappointed. (The ride listings in chapter 6, "Exploring Walt Disney World," note any minimum heights, as do the guide maps you can get at the parks.)

• **Take a Break**   The Disney parks have fabulous interactive **play areas** offering parents and young kids a break. By all means take advantage of them. Note that many of these kid zones are filled with water squirters and shallow pools, and most of the parks feature a fair number of water-related attractions, so getting wet is practically inevitable—at least for the kids. It's advisable to bring along a change of clothes or even a bathing suit. You can rent a locker ($10 or less) for storing the spares until you need them.

- **Show Time** Schedule an indoor, air-conditioned show two or three times a day, especially midafternoon in the summer. For all shows, arrive at least 20 minutes early to get the better seats, but not so early that the kids are tired of waiting (most waits are outside in the heat).

- **Snack Times** When dreaming of your vacation, you probably don't envision hours spent standing in lines, waiting and waiting (unless you have done this before, that is). It helps to store some lightweight **snacks** in a backpack, or in the stroller if you have one, especially when traveling with small children. This may save you some headaches, as kids get the hungriest just when you are the farthest from food. It will also be much healthier and will certainly save you money, as the parks' prices are quite high.

- **Bring Your Own?** While you will have to haul it to and from the car and on and off trams, trains, or monorails at Disney, having your own **stroller** can be a tremendous help. It will be with you when you need it—say, back in the hotel room as a highchair, or for an infant in a restaurant when a highchair is inappropriate. Remember to bring the right stroller, too. It should be lightweight, easy to fold and unfold with one hand, have a canopy, be able to recline for naps, and have plenty of storage space. The parks offer stroller rentals for around $10 to $31 per day; however these are often hard and uncomfortable (and rental fees could easily exceed the cost of a purchasing a stroller after just a few days). They do not recline and have little or no storage space for the gear that goes along with bringing the kids. They are good, however, if you have older kids who may just need an occasional break from walking. For infants and small toddlers, you may want to bring a snugly sling or back-pack-type carrier for use in traveling to and from parking lots and while you're standing in line for attractions (where strollers are not allowed). And while many parks now have a small number of infant-friendly strollers on hand, I still highly recommend bringing your own if your kids are younger than 3 or 4.

Most airlines require that an infant be 2 weeks old to travel. American and Continental require that the child be 7 days old. Alaska lets babies fly as soon as they're born. Bring a birth certificate for your newborn.

The practice of allowing children younger than 2 to ride for free on a parent's lap is still in effect; however, a new rule proposed by the FAA would require all children under 40 pounds to have their own tickets and be secured in a child safety seat, so be sure to double-check the rules when you book your flight.

Most major American airlines offer discounted infant tickets for children 2 or younger to make it more affordable for you to reserve a separate adjacent seat for your baby (and his safety seat).

If a seat adjacent to yours is available, your lap child can sit there free of charge. When you check in, ask if the flight is crowded. If it isn't, explain your situation to the agent, and ask if you can reserve two seats—or simply move to two empty adjacent seats once the plane is boarded. You might want to shop around before you buy your ticket and deliberately book a flight that's not very busy (though that's often difficult, given the destination). Ask the reservationist which flights tend to be most full, and avoid those if possible. Only one extra child is allowed in each row, however, due to the limited number of oxygen masks.

*Note:* Children riding for free will usually not be granted any baggage allowance.

## Child Seats: They're a Must

The FAA recommends that children under 20 pounds ride in a rear-facing child-restraint system; those who weigh 20 to 40 pounds should sit in a forward-facing child-restraint system. Children over 40 pounds should sit in a regular seat and wear a seat belt.

All child seats manufactured after 1985 are certified for airline use, but make sure your car seat will fit in an airline seat—it must be less than 16 inches wide. You may not use booster seats, seatless vests, or harness systems. Safety seats must be placed in window seats—except in exit rows, where they are prohibited, so as not to block the passage of other travelers in the case of an emergency.

The airlines themselves should carry child safety seats on board. Unfortunately, most don't. To make matters worse, overzealous flight attendants have been known to try to keep safety seats off planes. One traveler recounts in the November 2001 issue of *Consumer Reports Travel Letter* how a Southwest attendant attempted to block use of a seat because the red label certifying it as safe for airline use had flaked off. That traveler won her case by bringing the owner's manual and appealing to the pilot; you should do the same.

## 7 SPECIALIZED TRAVEL RESOURCES

### TRAVELERS WITH DISABILITIES

**ACCOMMODATIONS** Every hotel and motel in Florida is required by law to have a special room or rooms equipped for wheelchairs. A few have wheel-in showers. Walt Disney World's **Coronado Springs Resort** (✆ 407/934-7639 or 407/939-1000; www.disneyworld.com) has 99 rooms designed to accommodate guests with disabilities. Make your special needs known when making reservations at any hotel. For other information about special Disney rooms, call ✆ **407/939-7807.**

If you don't mind staying 10 to 15 minutes or so from Disney, check out one of the areas various vacation homes. **All Star Vacation Homes** is one of the best around (✆ **800/592-5568** or 407/997-0733; www.allstarvacationhomes.com), offering among other things, several handicapped-accessible homes that have multiple bedrooms, multiple baths (including accessible showers), full kitchens, and pools. Most cost less than $300 a night and are located in Kissimmee (though you'll find a handful of villas and townhomes located near I-Drive).

**TRANSPORTATION** Disney shuttle buses all accommodate wheelchairs, as does the monorail system and some of the water-craft that travel to the parks and resorts.

If you need to rent a wheelchair or electric scooter for your visit, **Walker Medical & Mobility Products** offers delivery to your room, and there's a model for guests who weigh as much as 375 pounds. These products fit into Disney's transports and monorails as well as rental cars. Get more information by calling ✆ **888/726-6837** or 407/331-9500, or on the Internet go to **www.walker mobility.com**. **CARE Medical Equipment** (✆ **800/741-2282** or 407/856-2273; www.caremedicalequipment.com) offers similar services.

**Disney** (✆ **407/934-7639**; www.disneyworld.com) offers wheelchair rentals at the parks, and, in more limited numbers, at the resorts. In addition, a very limited number of Electric Conve-nience Scooters are also available for rent at the parks. *Note:* Although the Segway is becoming increasingly popular as a mode of transportation for those with disabilities, Disney does not per-mit them inside any of their parks.

**IN THE PARKS** Many attractions at the parks, especially the newer ones, are designed to be accessible to a wide variety of guests. People with wheelchairs and their parties are often given preferen-tial treatment so they can avoid lines.

The available assistance is outlined in the guide maps you get as you enter the parks. All of the theme parks offer some parking close to the entrances for those with disabilities. Let the parking booth attendant know your needs, and you'll be directed to the appropriate spot. Wheelchair and electric cart rentals are available at most major attractions, but you'll be most comfortable in your chair or cart from home if you can bring it. Keep in mind, however, that wheelchairs wider than 24½ inches may be difficult to navigate through some attractions. And crowds may make it tough for any guest.

Disney's many services are detailed in each theme park's *Guide-book for Guests with Disabilities.* You can pick one up at Guest Relations near the front entrances to each of the parks. Also, you can call ✆ **407/934-7639** or 407/824-2222 for answers to any questions regarding special needs. The guide is also available online at Disney's website, **www.disneyworld.com** and **www.disney. go.com/disabilities**. For information regarding Telecommunications Devices for the Deaf (TDDs) call ⓒ **407/827-5141 (TTY).**

## FOR SINGLE PARENTS

Single parents face unique challenges when they travel with their children. **Parents without Partners** (ⓒ **800/637-7974;** www. parentswithoutpartners.org) provides links to numerous single-parent resources. Single mom Brenda Elwell's website, **www.singleparent travel.net**, is full of advice garnered from traveling around the world with her two children.

## FOR GAY & LESBIAN FAMILIES

The popularity of Orlando with gay and lesbian travelers, including families, parallels the growing number of same-sex households in the area. **Gay, Lesbian & Bisexual Community Services of Central Florida,** 934 N. Mills Ave., Orlando, FL 32803 (ⓒ **407/ 228-8272;** www.glbcc.org), is a great source of information on Central Florida. Welcome packets usually include the latest issue of the *Triangle,* a quarterly newsletter dedicated to gay and lesbian issues, and a calendar of events pertaining to the gay and lesbian community. Though not a tourist-specific packet, it includes information and ads for local gay and lesbian clubs. **Gay Orlando Network** (www.gayorlando.com) is another local resource.

The **International Gay and Lesbian Travel Association (IGLTA;** ⓒ **800/448-8550** or 954/630-1637; www.iglta.org) is the trade association for the gay and lesbian travel industry. It offers an online directory of gay- and lesbian-friendly travel businesses and tour operators.

## TRAVELING WITH PETS

For those of us who wouldn't dream of going on vacation without our pets, more and more lodgings are going the pet-friendly route. Be aware, however, policies vary from property to property in Orlando, so call ahead to find out the particulars of your hotel.

**Tips** **The Peripatetic Pet**

It is illegal in Florida to leave your pet inside a parked car, windows rolled down or not. The sweltering heat can easily kill an animal in only a few minutes. All of the major theme parks have kennel facilities available, so if you have brought your pet along, take advantage of these kennels.

Make sure your pet is wearing a name-tag that includes your name and phone number, as well as the phone number of a contact person who can take the call if your pet gets lost while you're away from home.

None of the Disney resorts allow animals (except service dogs) to stay on the premises or have their own kennels (the only exception being Disney's Fort Wilderness Resort and Campground, where you can have your pet at the full-hook-up campsites), but resort guests are welcome to board their animals overnight in kennel facilities at the Park's four (soon to be five) kennels.

An excellent resource is **www.petswelcome.com**, which dispenses medical tips, names of animal-friendly lodgings and campgrounds, and lists of kennels and veterinarians. Also check out **www.dogfriendly.com**, which features links to Orlando accommodations, eateries, attractions, and parks that welcome canine companions.

For more resources about traveling with pets, go to **www.frommers.com/planning**. You can also refer to "Pet Care" under "Services & Facilities" for each individual park in chapter 6, "Exploring Walt Disney World."

# 8 SUSTAINABLE TOURISM

While sustainable travel may not be the first thing you think of when heading to the theme-park capital of the world, Orlando

**Tips** **"Green" Hotels**

Quite a number of Orlando hotels have received "green" certification by the Florida Department of Environmental Protection and have been designated as Green Lodge hotels. To be considered for the certification, hotels must adhere to a set list of requirements, including conservation of water through the use of low-flow plumbing fixtures, a linen reuse program, and the use of energy-efficient and programmable thermostats. Waste-reduction criteria must also be met. All Green Lodges must also use green cleaning supplies and high-efficiency air filters.

Green Lodge resorts can (and do) range from mom-and-pop motels to five-star luxury resorts in Orlando. For more on the program and a complete list of the hotels in and around Orlando that are green (there are several, including all official WDW resorts and all official Universal resorts), go to **www.dep.state.fl.us/GreenLodging**.

takes the environment quite seriously: understandable for an area that's impacted so heavily by the millions of tourists who visit from around the world (a number that far exceeds the number of actual area residents). As the city's largest employers, Disney, Universal, and SeaWorld (among others) actively encourage eco-friendly practices—on their own part as well as on the part of the millions of guests who pass through their gates, eat at their restaurants, and stay at their hotels.

Disney, in addition to ensuring that its entire collection of hotels are "green" certified properties, has announced that over the next 10 years it will decrease greenhouse emissions by half (though the goal is to eliminate them altogether down the road) and will decrease its electrical use by 10%. Other lofty goals include the reduction of solid waste (cut by 50% by the year 2013).

Using public transportation (most notably Disney's vast array of buses, monorails, and water taxis; Universal's water taxis and buses; International Dr.'s I-Ride Trolley system, and so forth) contributes to getting more cars off the street, making for cleaner air. In Orlando, it's even possible to hire a pedicab; the **Redi Pedi Pedicab** (✆ 407/403-5511); and **5 Star Pedicab** (✆ 407/566-7527) are the two largest companies serving the Orlando area.

# 9 VACATION PACKAGES

The number and diversity of package tours to Orlando is staggering. But you can save money if you're willing to do the research. Head to **www.disneyworld.com** (where you'll find loads of information and can book a package as well). Disney's array of choices can include airfare, accommodations on or off Disney property, theme-park passes, a rental car, meals, a Disney cruise, and/or a stay at Disney's beach resorts in Vero Beach or Hilton Head, South Carolina. Some packages are tied to a season, while others are for special-interest vacationers, including golfers, honeymooners, or spa aficionados. For more information, or to book a Disney vacation package, call ✆ **407/939-6244.**

One good source of package deals is the airlines themselves. Most major airlines offer air/land packages to Orlando, including **American Airlines Vacations** (✆ **800/321-2121;** www.aavacations. com), **Delta Vacations** (✆ **800/654-6559;** www.deltavacations. com), **Continental Airlines Vacations** (✆ **800/301-3800;** www. covacations.com), and **United Vacations** (✆ **888/854-3899;** www. unitedvacations.com). Several big **online travel agencies**—Expedia, Travelocity, Orbitz, Site59, and Lastminute.com—also do a brisk business in Orlando packages.

**Touraine Travel** (✆ **617/426-4418;** www.tourainetravel.com) is a source of packages to Disney.

# 10 STAYING CONNECTED

## TELEPHONES

Generally, hotel surcharges in Orlando on long-distance and local calls are astronomical (check the telephone information card often found on or next to the phone in your room for the lowdown on all the costs involved), so, unless it's unavoidable, you're better off using your **cellphone** (just be sure to check your coverage area, roaming fees, and, if required, international calling capabilities before leaving home) or even a **public pay telephone** to make a phone call. Many public pay phones at airports now accept American Express, MasterCard, and Visa credit cards. **Local calls** made from pay phones in most locales cost 25¢ to 35¢ (and they don't give change).

Most long-distance and international calls can be dialed directly from any phone, though most Orlando hotels require a credit card imprint upon check-in against possible room charges—including use of the phone. **For calls within the United States and to Canada,** dial 1 followed by the area code and the seven-digit number. And note that in Orlando you have to remember to dial all 10 digits (including the area code) even if you're just calling across the street.

For **reversed-charge or collect calls,** and for person-to-person calls (also an expensive way to call when traveling), dial the number 0, then the area code, and the number; an operator will come on the line, and you should specify whether you are calling collect, person-to-person, or both. If your operator-assisted call is international, ask for the overseas operator.

 **Tips** **Don't Forget the 407**

**Local calls** in Orlando require that you dial the area code **(407)** followed by the seven-digit local number, even when calling just across the street.

For **local directory assistance** ("information"), dial ℂ **411;** for long-distance information, dial 1, then the appropriate area code, and 555-1212.

## INTERNET & E-MAIL
### With Your Own Computer

Most Orlando hotels (especially the larger area resorts) offer Wi-Fi access at least in public areas such as the lobby, lounges and even some restaurants, with a few providing in-room wireless access. To find public Wi-Fi hotspots in Orlando, go to **www.jiwire.com**; its Hotspot Finder holds the world's largest directory of public wireless hotspots.

For dial-up access, most business-class hotels in Orlando offer dataports for laptop modems, and an ever-increasing number of them offer free high-speed Internet access. For a list of Orlando hotels wired for Internet access, check out **www.wiredhotels.com**. Charges to connect (while often free at many budget and moderately priced hotels) can run upwards of $10 per each 24-hour period you're connected. Disney offers high-speed access to guests at all of its resorts, and Wi-Fi access at select resorts.

### Without Your Own Computer

At Walt Disney World, there is an Internet cafe inside **Disney-Quest.** You can send e-mail at **Innoventions in Epcot** (p. 143), though you have to pay the park admission fees to use the Web terminals. Payphones with touch-screen displays offering Internet access have been installed at locations throughout Walt Disney World; you can access your e-mail for 25¢ a minute with a 4-minute minimum.

Many hotels have either a business center with computers available (some can even be rented and taken back to your room) or, in some instances, a computer located in the lobby for guest use. Some even have WebTV available in the guest rooms, where a keyboard works in conjunction with the television (just don't count on it being as user friendly—or as speedy as a laptop or PC), or an actual in-room PC. In either case, there will likely (but not always) be (often exorbitant) fees for using them.

# Getting to Know Walt Disney World

It's hard to believe that Walt Disney World (WDW) first opened its gates to the public just under 40 years ago. I doubt anyone could have imagined the incredible transformation that followed in the wake of the Magic Kingdom's 1971 debut. Orlando has evolved from a relatively quiet southern farming community into an international vacation destination.

An incredible array of recreational activities, shopping and dining experiences, and world-class accommodations await those who visit, and it's all set right in the middle of the natural beauty of Central Florida.

## 1 ORIENTATION

### VISITOR INFORMATION

Once you've arrived, you can stop in at the **Orlando/Orange County Convention & Visitors Bureau (Orlando CVB),** 8723 International Dr., Ste. 101, Orlando; however, it's best to call ahead (© **800/972-3304** or 407/363-5872; www.orlandoinfo. com) for information on the area's offerings. Staffers at the CVB can help answer your questions, as well as hand out maps, brochures, and coupons good for discounts or freebies. It's worth a visit even if you take the advice in chapter 2, "Planning Your Trip to Walt Disney World," and send for them before arriving. The CVB sells discount tickets to several attractions. Only Disney's 4-day or longer passes are discounted with savings from $5 to $15 depending on the ticket. The CVB's multilingual staff can make dinner reservations and hotel referrals for you. The CVB is open daily from 8:30am to 7:30pm, except Christmas. From I-4, take exit 74A east 2 blocks, turn south on International Drive and continue 1 mile. The center is on the left, at the corner of I-Drive and Austrian Row.

## CITY LAYOUT

Though Walt Disney World and Orlando are often considered synonymous (surprise!), WDW isn't situated in Orlando. It's actually located southwest of the city in Lake Buena Vista (and is a municipal entity in its own right).

**Lake Buena Vista** actually encompasses all of WDW, but also includes much of the area bordering the resort. Here you can find the "official" (but not Disney-owned) hotels situated along Hotel Plaza Boulevard. The area along 535 (known locally as Apopka–Vineland), is home to its own share of resorts and restaurants. Though the region is bustling, many of its resorts, restaurants, and shops are set along alcoves and tree-lined side streets, far from the main thoroughfare, to maintain a quieter, more charming atmosphere.

Orlando's major artery is Interstate 4. Locals call it the **I-4** or that *#@$*%^#!!* highway! It runs diagonally across the state (though directional signs are always marked east or west) from Tampa to Daytona Beach. The exits along this route will take you to Disney, Universal, SeaWorld, International Drive, U.S. 192, Kissimmee, Lake Buena Vista, and north to downtown Orlando and Winter Park. Most exits are well marked, but construction is common and exit numbers have been changed through the years. If you get directions by exit number, always ask the name of the road to help avoid getting lost. (Cellphone users can dial ✆ **511** to get a report of I-4 delays.)

The **Florida Turnpike,** a toll road, crosses I-4 and links with I-75 to the north and Miami to the south. **U.S. 192/Irlo Bronson Memorial Highway** is a major east–west artery that reaches from Kissimmee to U.S. 27, crossing I-4 near World Drive, the main Walt Disney World entrance road. The **Beachline Expressway** (Hwy. 528; previously the Bee Line Expwy.), also a toll road, goes

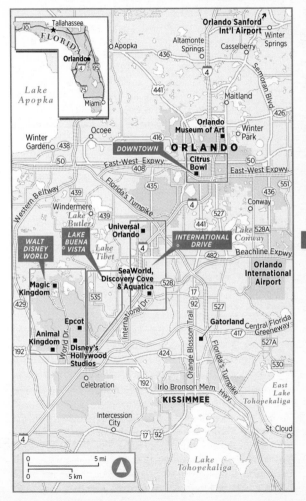

east from I-4 past Orlando International Airport to Cape Canaveral and Kennedy Space Center. The **East–West Expressway** (also known as Hwy. 408) is a toll road that can be helpful in bypassing surface traffic in the downtown area. The **417,** also a toll road, runs from north of the Orlando International Airport to I-4 just below U.S. 192. This route is a good alternative to I-4 if you are staying on the lower end of International Drive, World Center Drive, or areas east of the I-4, as it is far less traveled than the main highway.

I-4 and Highway 535 roughly bound **Walt Disney World** to the east (the latter is also a northern boundary) and U.S. 192/Irlo Bronson Memorial Highway bounds it to the south. World Drive is WDW's main north–south artery. Epcot Center Drive (Hwy. 536/the south end of International Dr.) and Buena Vista Drive cut across the complex in a more or less east–west direction; the two roads cross at Bonnet Creek Parkway. Despite a reasonably good highway system and explicit signs, it's easy to get lost or miss a turn here—even if you think you know the roads. I've gotten lost or passed an exit on Disney property at least once or twice on every trip. Again, pay attention and drive carefully. Don't panic or pull across several lanes of traffic to make an exit, especially once you're on Disney property—there's always another exit just ahead where you can turn around. All roads lead to the parks, and you'll soon find another sign directing you to the same place. It may take a bit longer, but Goofy will still be there.

## 2 GETTING AROUND

In a city that thrives on its attractions, you won't find it difficult to get around—especially if you have a car. If you're traveling outside the tourist areas, avoid the 7 to 9am and 4 to 7pm rush if at all possible. Commuter traffic (recently ranked as fourth-worst in the nation) can be bad anywhere, but here the complication of tourist traffic makes it even more of a headache. And don't expect weekends to be any better—the locals who run the hotels, restaurants, and attractions still have to get to work, making commuter traffic a 7-day-a-week problem.

Disney resorts and official hotels offer unlimited free transportation via bus, monorail, ferry, or water taxi to all WDW properties throughout the day, and at times, well into the evening. If, however, you want to venture elsewhere (say, to Universal or SeaWorld), you'll just have to pay extra to do so.

If you're staying at the Disney resorts, using the system can save you money on a rental car, insurance, and gas, as well as all those parking fees ($14 a day at the WDW theme parks, though Disney resort guests are exempt from parking charges). The drawback, however, is that you're at the mercy of Disney's schedules, which are often slow and, at times, *very* indirect; bus trips from the outlying resorts (especially Fort Wilderness) to the various parks (and vice versa) can take over an hour during peak times.

Pick up a map when you land at the Guest Services desks at any of the Disney resorts and theme parks, or download a more generic map at **www.disneyworld.com**.

The best rule when using Disney transportation: Ask the driver or someone at your hotel's front desk to help you take the most direct route. Keep asking questions along the way. Unlike missing a highway exit, missing a bus stop means you may reach pension age before you reach your destination.

## BY CAR

Whether or not to rent a car while in Orlando is one of the most important decisions you will make when planning your trip (just behind selecting your hotel). First, think about your vacation plans. If you're planning on going beyond the boundaries of Disney to Universal, SeaWorld, or anywhere along I-Drive, a rental car is a necessity. If you want to head out in the evenings to smaller attractions, dinner shows, or other activities not located within the realm of Disney, a car will definitely allow you the most flexibility. If you plan to limit your vacation only to WDW, then a car might prove an extra and unnecessary expense ("might" being the operative word here).

If you've decided to stay right on Disney property, the question to ask yourself is how, exactly, will you get to the parks? If the

**Tips** **Look Both Ways**

Traveling on foot anywhere in Orlando, most especially on International Drive, can be tricky. If you have to walk across a parking lot or street, *be careful.* The Surface Transportation Policy Project's pedestrian safety report has named Orlando the most dangerous city in the country for pedestrians. Drivers are paying far more attention to their maps and street signs, not to the people running in front of them.

Magic Kingdom is accessible only by taking a bus, switching to the monorail, and then catching a ferry, you may want to opt for a car. The least expensive properties, the All-Star resorts, are among the farthest from the Disney parks. Wait times between buses can be considerable, if not unendurable.

During peak hours in the busiest seasons, you may have trouble getting a seat on the bus, so keep that in mind if you're traveling with seniors or companions with disabilities. Also, if you're bringing along children and strollers, consider the frustration factor of loading and unloading strollers and all of the paraphernalia that comes with them on and off buses, ferries, and trams.

A car may drastically cut the commute time between the parks and hotels not directly on the monorail routes, so decide how much your time is worth and how much the car will cost plus the $14 per day theme-park parking charge (Disney resort guests, however, are exempt from the parking fees) before making a decision about renting.

**All of the major car-rental companies** are represented in Orlando and maintain desks at or near the airport. Many agencies provide discount coupons in publications targeted at tourists, though you should keep in mind that AAA discounts and online offers are often better. Also, it never hurts to ask about specials. Be advised that many rental agencies in Florida will rent only to drivers 21 and older, and that drivers younger than age 25 may have to pay a young renter's fee of up to $25 a day! *Note:* Disney has an **Alamo** car-rental desk (© **800/327-2996**) right on property, so if you're interested in renting for only a few days instead of your entire vacation, this may be a good option for you.

## Car-Rental Insurance

Car-rental insurance usually costs $25 or more a day. If you hold a private auto insurance policy, you are **probably** covered in the U.S. for loss or damage to the car, as well as liability in case a passenger is injured. The credit card you use to rent the car also may provide some coverage. Double-check with your insurance company and your credit-card company regarding what may or may not be covered on both ends. *Note:* Many car-rental companies now charge steep out-of-service fees, if the car is out of commission for any reason after its return. Also note that some car-rental companies have been known to lie about the amount of coverage you need to get you to sign up for policies that make them quite a bit of profit. Always do your homework on what is and isn't covered by you policy before you get to the rental counter.

Car-rental insurance probably does not cover liability if you cause an accident (some companies may, however, offer supplemental liability insurance for an additional daily fee). Check your own auto insurance policy, the rental company policy, and your credit card coverage for the extent of coverage: Is your destination covered? Are other drivers covered? How much liability is covered if a passenger is injured? (If you rely on your credit card for coverage, you may want to bring a second credit card with you. Damages may be charged to your card, and you may find yourself stranded with no money.) You don't need any surprises spoiling your vacation, so look at your coverage before reaching the rental counter.

## Driving in Town

SPEED LIMITS   Obey posted speed limits. On highways and interstates, they're usually 55 or 65 mph but as high as 70 mph in some rural areas. In residential areas, 30 or 35 mph is usually the case. *Note:* The corridor between the attractions and downtown

Orlando is a speed trap with fines for speeding starting at $80 (and reaching as high as $305). Fines double in construction areas and school zones.

**SEAT BELTS**    Seat belts are required for all passengers. Children ages 3 and younger must be buckled into a car seat, children ages 4 and 5 must be in a safety restraint (whether a car seat, booster seat, or seat belt). Police will issue tickets to parents who don't put their children in the proper restraints while driving. Many car-rental agencies offer car seat rentals; though if you will be here for more than just a few days, you may want to consider bringing your own as the rental cost will almost add up to the price of a new car seat.

**DRINKING & DRIVING**    Don't. It's that simple. Florida's rules are strict and strictly enforced. If you're planning to drink (alcohol that is), especially after an exhausting day in the theme parks, designate a sober driver or find an alternative means of transportation (there are plenty of options). Some clubs even provide free soft drinks to designated drivers. If you don't obey the law, your accommodations may change from a four-star hotel room to a Florida jail cell in short order.

**DEFENSIVE DRIVING**    Drive with extra care in tourist-heavy areas. It's not uncommon for drivers to make sudden turns or to slow down unexpectedly when reading road signs. Assume all other drivers have no idea where they're going—which is often close to the truth—and you'll do fine. If you miss your exit, don't panic—there are plenty others (especially around Disney) that can get you where you want to go.

**DRIVING IN THE RAIN**    Watch for a hazardous condition where oil on the road creates slick patches when the road gets wet. Rainstorms in Florida are intense and frequent; they're almost a daily occurrence in summer. Exercise extreme caution and drive in the far right lane when driving much slower than the speed limit. Don't pull off onto the shoulder of the road. If visibility is especially poor, pull off at the first exit and wait out the storm; they seldom last more than an hour. Florida law requires drivers to turn on their headlights whenever they turn on their windshield wipers.

**IF YOU GET LOST**   Exit numbers continue to change and signs continue to be confusing. On interstates or Orlando's toll roads, don't try a U-turn across the grassy median. Go to the next exit and reenter the highway by accessing the on-ramp near where you get off. Avoid pulling over to ask directions from people on the street. Instead, stop at a convenience store or gas station and ask the clerk. Don't forget, you can get maps ahead of time from the Orlando CVB (p. 33). If you are renting a car, most agencies will provide a map (some even provide computer-generated directions). Some rental-car agencies offer GPS navigational systems with their rentals as an add-on; inquire when you rent your car.

**SAFETY WHILE DRIVING**   Question your rental agency about personal safety or ask for a brochure on traveler safety tips when you pick up your car. Obtain written directions from the agency or a map with the route marked in red, showing how to get to your destination. And, if possible, arrive and depart during daylight hours.

If you drive off a highway and end up in a dodgy-looking neighborhood, turn around and leave the area as quickly as possible. If you have an accident, even on the highway, stay in your car with the doors locked until you assess the situation or until the police arrive. If you're bumped from behind on the street or are involved in a minor accident with no injuries, and the situation appears to be suspicious, motion to the other driver to follow you. Never open the window or get out of your car in such situations. Go directly to the nearest police station, well-lit service station, or 24-hour store.

If you see someone else on the road indicating a need for help, don't stop. Take note of the location, and call the police by dialing ℂ **911** to make them aware of the situation.

Park in well-lit, well-traveled areas whenever possible. Keep your doors locked, whether you're inside the car or not. Look around before you get out and never leave packages, pocketbooks, or any kind of valuables in sight. Although theme park lots are patrolled, it's best to secure your valuables at all times. For an added measure of security, you can always lock things in the lockers available near all of the park entrances. If it is an item you really don't need with you that day, use the hotel safe for storage and don't even bring it along.

## BY BUS

Stops for the **Lynx** bus system (© **407/841-5969;** www.golynx. com) are marked with a paw print. It will get you to Disney, Universal, and I-Drive (one-way fare is $2 adults, $1 kids 7-18, kids 6 and younger ride free; express passes and daylong passes are available as well), but it's generally not very tourist-friendly.

**Mears Transportation** (© **407/423-5566;** www.mears transportation.com) operates buses to all the major attractions, including Kennedy Space Center, Universal Studios, SeaWorld, and Busch Gardens (yes, in Tampa), among others. Rates vary based on where you are going and where you are coming from, so call ahead for the particulars. Many of the area hotels use Mears for their shuttle service to the parks and attractions. If your hotel does not provide free shuttle service, make sure you compare the costs of taking shuttles to the cost of renting a car before deciding on your transportation; the car will often be the cheaper way to go.

## BY TAXI

Taxis will line up in front of major hotels in addition to a few smaller properties. If you wish, you can also call **Yellow Cab** (© **407/699-9999**) and **Ace Metro** (© **407/855-1111**) on your own. Both are good choices; however, rates can run as high as $3.25 for the first mile, $1.75 per mile thereafter, though occasionally you can get a flat rate if you ask. In general, cabs are economical only if you have four or five people aboard and aren't going very far or very many times. You could actually rent your own car (depending on the model) for the price of just a few taxi rides.

# Where to Stay

**Just a few years back, there seemed to be no end to** Orlando's hotel boom. Almost 4,000 new rooms were added every year through 2000, and then things began to slow down. By 2007 tourism was once again thriving, and the city's existing inventory saw the largest jump in nearly a decade with roughly 5,000 rooms added in 2008 alone. The year 2009 brought with it an additional 2,558 rooms, while just over 1,700 were added in 2010. New construction, however, has all but come to a halt—a reflection of the latest economic downturn. All in all, the Orlando area now boasts more than 116,000 rooms, including scores of places located in or near the major-league tourist draws: Walt Disney World, Universal Orlando, SeaWorld, and the rest of International Drive. Disney alone claims 35 resorts, timeshares, and "official" hotels.

## HOW TO CHOOSE A HOTEL & SAVE MONEY

All of the rates cited in the following pages are what are called "rack rates." That means they're typical prices listed in the hotel brochures or the ones that hotel clerks give over the telephone. You can almost always negotiate a better price by purchasing package deals, by assuring the clerks they can do better, or by mentioning to the clerk that you belong to one of several organizations that receive a discount (such as AARP, AAA, the armed services, or a labor union). The Orlando Magicard can save you plenty of cash as well. Even the type of credit card you use could get you a **5% to 10% discount** at some of the larger chains. Any discount you get will help ease the impact of local resort taxes, which aren't included in the quoted rates. *These taxes will add up to 12.5% to your bill, depending on where you're staying.*

WDW's 2011 value seasons or lowest rates are generally available from January 3 to February 11, August 15 to September 30, and November 28 to December 16. Regular season rates are available from April 11 to June 3 and October 1 to November 24. Easter rates run from March 28 to April 10. Summer rates (only at Disney's "value" and "moderate" resorts) run from June 4 to August 14. Peak rates apply from February 15 to March 27, and holiday rates from November 24 to November 27 and December 17 through December 31. Be aware, however, that Disney's new pricing schedule breaks down seasonal rates even further to include specific weekends and holidays such as Presidents' Day, Independence Day, and MLK Day, among others.

If you're not renting a car or staying at a Walt Disney World resort, be sure to ask when booking your room if the hotel or motel offers **transportation to the theme parks** and, if so, whether there's a charge and exactly what it is. Some hotels and motels offer free service with their own shuttles (listed in the reviews in this chapter). Others use Mears Transportation (see "Getting Around," in chapter 3), and rates can be as high as $18 per person round-trip (some hotels make these arrangements for you; others require you to do it). On the other hand, if you have a vehicle, expect to pay $14 a day to park it at Disney.

If you stay at a WDW resort or one of Disney's "official" hotels, transportation is complimentary within WDW.

In or out of Walt Disney World, if you book your hotel as part of a **package** (see "Vacation Packages," in chapter 2, for more details), you'll likely enjoy some type of savings. The **Walt Disney Travel Company** (© 407/939-7796) offers a number of Disney resort packages.

Outside Disney, you'll probably be quoted a rate better than the rack rates contained in the following listings, but you should try to bargain even further to ensure you get the best rates possible. Ask about discounts for students, government employees, seniors, military, firefighters, police, AFL–CIO, corporate clients, and, again, AARP or AAA, holders of the Orlando Magicard, even frequent traveler programs (whether you have hotel or airline membership). Special Internet-only discounts and packages may also be featured on hotel websites, especially those of the larger chains. Never come to Orlando without a reservation: Taking chances on your negotiating skills is one thing; taking chances on room availability is quite another. Orlando is a year-round destination, with a heavy convention and business trade, and international vacationers flock here during periods when domestic travelers aren't.

## RESERVATION SERVICES

**Florida Hotel Network** (© 800/293-2419; www.floridahotel network.com), **Central Reservation Service** (© 800/555-7555 or 407/740-6442; www.crshotels.com), and **Hotels.com** (© 800/ 246-8357; www.hotels.com) are three other services that can help with room reservations and other kinds of reservations in Central Florida. **HotelKingdom.com** (© 877/766-6787 or 407/294-9600; www.hotelkingdom.com) is also a good source of room or vacation rental bargains. You can also book Disney World hotels directly by calling © **407/934-7639** or visiting **www.disney world.com**.

## HOW TO USE THIS CHAPTER

Unlike other Florida tourist areas, there are few under–$60 motels that meet the standards demanded for listing in this book. That's why I've raised the price bar. The ones in the **inexpensive** category charge an average of less than $90 per night for a double room. Those offering $90 to $180 rooms make up the **moderate** category; and anything more than $180 is listed as **expensive.** Any included extras (such as breakfast) are listed for each property. Keep in mind that rates are per night double unless otherwise noted, and they don't include hotel taxes of up to 12.5%. Also, most Orlando hotels and motels let **kids younger than 12 (and usually younger than 17) stay free** with a parent or guardian if you don't exceed maximum room occupancy. But to be safe, ask when booking your room.

- **Best for Families:** Every Disney resort caters to families, with special menus for kids, video-game arcades, free transportation to the parks, extensive recreational facilities, and, in some cases, character meals. Some, however, stand out in particular among the others. **Disney's Old Key West Resort** (✆ **407/934-7639** or 407/827-7700) offers the relaxed, laid-back charm of the Florida Keys and some of the best rooms on Disney property for families. Camping at the remote and wooded campgrounds of **Disney's Fort Wilderness Resort & Campground** (p. 59; ✆ **407/934-7639** or 407/824-2900) makes for a more down-to-earth family experience. To enjoy wilderness of a different kind, try **Disney's Animal Kingdom Lodge** (p. 50; ✆ **407/934-7639** or 407/938-3000), where the animals of the African savanna seemingly come right to your doorstep. If you prefer the rustic and woodsy feel of the Pacific Northwest's national parks, head to the **Wilderness Lodge** (p. 51; ✆ **407/934-7639** or 407/824-3200). Outside the House of Mouse, **Nickelodeon Family Suites** (p. 69; ✆ **877/642-5543** or 407/387-5437) features two- and three-bedroom Kid Suites, multilevel water slides, extensive play areas, and an all-Nickelodeon decor.

- **Best Inexpensive Hotels:** That's easy: If you're going to stay on WDW property, you can't beat the prices at **Disney's All-Star Movies Resort, Disney's All-Star Music Resort, Disney's All-Star Sports Resort,** and **Disney's Pop Century Resort** (beginning p. 57). To book a room at any of Disney's inexpensive resorts, call ✆ **407/934-7639.**

- **Best Pool:** The super kid-friendly water park–style pools at the **Nickelodeon Family Suites** (p. 69; ✆ **877/642-5543** or 407/3 87-5437) have towers, slides, climbing nets, miniflumes, and more.

WHERE TO STAY

4

THE BEST HOTEL BETS

# 2 THE PERKS OF STAYING WITH MICKEY

The decision on whether to bunk with the Mouse is one of the first you'll have to make when planning your vacation. The following amenities are included at all Disney resorts; **some** are offered by the "official" hotels, but be sure to ask when booking:

- Guests get free transportation from Orlando International Airport via Disney transportation to their Disney resort using **Magical Express** (the program is currently slated to run through 2011). Not only does the shuttle service get Disney resort guests to their hotels, but it also delivers their baggage straight from the plane to their room, allowing them to bypass baggage claim! As an added bonus, guests can check their luggage and print out boarding passes for their return trip before leaving their Disney resort (though you'll have to prepay any airline luggage fees if you use the system—ask at your resort if you want to take advantage of this feature), allowing them to skip the long lines at the airport. Currently only select airlines participate in the program.

- Unlimited **free transportation** on the **Walt Disney World Transportation System**'s buses, monorails, ferries, or water taxis to and from the four WDW parks, from 2 hours prior to opening until 2 hours after closing. Free transportation is also provided to and from Typhoon Lagoon, Blizzard Beach, and the WDW resorts. Three of them—the Polynesian, Grand Floridian, and Contemporary resorts—are located on the Disney monorail system. The transportation services offered can save money you might otherwise spend on a rental car, parking, and shuttles. It also means you're guaranteed admission to all of the parks, even during peak times when parking lots sometimes fill to capacity.

- Kids younger than 17 **stay free** in their parent's room, and reduced-price children's menus are available in most restaurants.

- Character breakfasts and/or dinners at select restaurants.

- The **Extra Magic Hour** (p. 130).
- A **Lobby Concierge** (replacing the old Guest Services desk), where you can buy tickets to all Disney parks and attractions—without standing in long lines at the parks—and get information on dining, recreation, and everything Disney.
- WDW has some of the **best swimming pools** in Orlando and most are zero-entry or zero-grade pools, meaning there's a gradual slope into the water on at least one side rather than only a step down.
- On-premises car rental is available at the Magic Kingdom Auto Plaza through Alamo (© **407/824-3470**).
- Disney's **refillable mug program** lets you buy—for around $13.50—a bottomless souvenir mug for soda, coffee, tea, and/or cocoa at its resorts. The offer is for the length of your stay, but it isn't transferable to the theme parks. You can use it only at the property at which it is bought, with the exception of the three All-Star resorts, where the mug is transferable between each property. A similar program is available at Disney's two water parks, but again, they're not transferable beyond the park where they were purchased and aren't valid beyond the day they are purchased.
- Resort guests can **charge most purchases** (including meals) made anywhere inside WDW to their room. In most cases, purchases made inside the theme parks can be delivered to your resort at no extra charge.

But there are also disadvantages to staying with the Mouse:

- The complimentary **Walt Disney World Transportation System** can be *excruciatingly time consuming*. There are times when you have to take a ferry to catch a bus to get on the monorail to reach your hotel. The system makes a circuit but may not necessarily take the most direct path for you. It can take up to an hour or more to get to a place that's right across the lagoon from you.
- That free **Magical Express shuttle system** to and from the airport isn't perfect. Luggage delivery may take up to several hours, leaving you with only the clothes on your back (and whatever you packed in your carry-on) until it arrives. And departure shuttles (from your resort to the Orlando International Airport)

are scheduled several hours in advance of your flight (thanks in part to the numerous resort stops it makes before getting on its way), ensuring that you'll wait at the airport far longer than you would have to otherwise.

Also note that though the Magical Express service is provided by Disney, the airlines, unfortunately, still have a say in the matter. Changes to baggage policies (which vary by airline) have now spilled over to Disney's Magical Express. Though guests can still check their bags via the resort airline service, those with more than the allotted number of "free" bags will either have to call ahead (to the airline check-in service ☎ **407/824-1231**) to pay the additional fee (by credit card only) or check the additional pieces at the airport.

- Resort rates are around 20% to 30% higher than comparable hotels and motels away from the parks.
- Without a car or another means to get off the property, you'll either be resigned to paying Disney's higher prices or paying for shuttles to get to Orlando's other offerings.

## WALT DISNEY WORLD CENTRAL RESERVATIONS OFFICE (CRO) & WALT DISNEY TRAVEL COMPANY

To book a room or package at Disney's resorts, campgrounds, and "official" hotels through the **Walt Disney World Travel Company,** contact the **Central Reservations Office (CRO),** P.O. Box 10000, Lake Buena Vista, FL 32830-1000 (☎ **407/934-7639;** www.disneyworld.com).

CRO can recommend accommodations suited to your price range and specific needs. But the staffers who answer the phones usually don't volunteer information about a better deal or a special *unless you ask.* Be sure to inquire about Disney's numerous package plans, which can include meals, tickets, recreation, and other features. The right package can save you money and time if you use all of its features (there's no sense in paying for something you won't use); having a comprehensive game plan in place is helpful in computing the cost of your vacation in advance.

# 3 WHERE TO STAY IN WALT DISNEY WORLD

The resorts in this section are either Disney-owned or "official" Disney hotels that offer many of the same perks. All are on the Disney Transportation System, which means those of you who don't want to venture too far (and are okay with the occasional scheduling inconvenience) will be able to do without a car. If you do decide to bring or rent a car, you'll get free parking at your hotel and at the Disney parks.

If you decide that Disney is your destination, come up with a short list of preferred places to stay, and then call CRO (© **407/934-7639**) for up-to-the-minute rates. Web surfers can get information at **www.disneyworld.com**.

Prices in the following listings reflect the range available at each resort when this guide was published. Rates vary depending on season and room location, but the numbers should help you determine which places fit your budget.

*Note:* Most hotels and resorts, Disney or otherwise, have cribs (or portable cribs) available (though limited in number) at no extra charge. Rollaways or cots are usually available as well; however, many resorts will charge around $10 to $25 per night to use them. Refrigerators (mini ones, anyway) are sometimes available, though some hotels may charge up to $15 per night for the privilege. All Orlando hotels also offer at least some nonsmoking rooms, and *all of Disney's hotels went smoke free* (except for some designated outdoor areas) on June 1, 2007.

## EXPENSIVE

**Disney's Animal Kingdom Lodge** ★★★ **Kids** The feel of an African game-reserve lodge immediately surrounds you upon entering the grand stories-high lobby, which features a thatched roof and ornate shield chandeliers. The resort's *kraal* design (a semicircular layout) ensures most rooms overlook the 30-acre savanna, allowing guests an occasional view of the birds, giraffes,

> (**Tips**)    **A Night Out**
>
> Several of the higher-priced Disney resorts—including Ani-
> mal Kingdom Lodge and Wilderness Lodge—have super-
> vised child care, usually from 4 or 4:30pm to midnight
> daily ($11.25 per child 4–12, per hour, dinner and activities
> included; ℭ **407/939-3463**). Disney also offers in-room
> sitters through **Kid's Nite Out** (ℭ **407/827-5444;** www.
> kidsniteout.com).

and array of other African animals that call the savanna home
(rooms without the savanna view will save a few extra dollars; you
can get the scenery for free through large picture windows in the
lobby and from a nature trail set behind the pool area). Families
will appreciate the array of unique activities including storytelling
by the fire, singalongs, and more. Typical rooms are slightly smaller
than those at Disney's other "Deluxe" resorts, but the distinctive
theme and spectacular surroundings are unparalleled, making a
stay here well worth the slightly tighter squeeze. The lodge is adjacent to Animal Kingdom, but most everything else on WDW
property is quite a distance away.

2901 Osceola Pkwy., Bay Lake, FL 32830. ℭ **407/934-7639** or 407/938-3000.
Fax 407/939-4799. www.disneyworld.com. 1,293 units. $240–$580 double;
$415–$2,820 concierge level; $760–$2,990 suite; $275–$–$2,260 villas. Extra
person $25. Children 17 and younger stay free in parent's room. AE, DC, DISC,
MC, V. Self-parking free; valet parking $12. **Amenities:** 2 restaurants; cafe;
lounge; babysitting; supervised children's program; concierge; concierge-level
rooms; health club & limited spa; heated outdoor pool; kids' pool; room service;
WDW Transportation System; transportation to non-Disney parks for a fee.
*In room:* A/C, TV, DVD (concierge-level), fridge (free, upon request), hair dryer,
Internet (fee), microwave (concierge-level).

**Disney's Wilderness Lodge** ★★★ (**Kids**)  The geyser out
back, the mammoth stone hearth in the lobby, and bunk beds for
the kids are just a few reasons this resort is a favorite of families.
Surrounded by 56 acres of oaks and pines, it offers a woodsy and

# Walt Disney World & Lake Buena Vista Accommodations & Dining

**4**

## WHERE TO DINE

1900 Park Fare **3**
Artist Point **5**
Boatwright's Dining Hall **25**
Boma **31**
California Grill **4**
Cape May Café **29**
Chef Mickey's **4**
The Crab House **12**
Disney's Spirit of Aloha Dinner Show **2**
ESPN Club **28**
Flying Fish Café **28**
Hemingway's **13**
Hoop-Dee-Doo Musical Revue **6**
Jiko—The Cooking Place **31**
Kouzzinas **28**
Mikado Japanese Steakhouse **22**
'Ohana **2**
Rainforest Café **32**
Romano's Macaroni Grill **8**
Todd English's bluezoo **30**
Whispering Canyon Café **5**

## LAKE BUENA VISTA HOTELS

Embassy Suites Lake Buena Vista **10**
Hampton Inn Orlando/Lake Buena Vista **11**
Hawthorn Suites Lake Buena Vista **11**
Holiday Inn SunSpree Resort Lake Buena Vista **18**
Lake Buena Vista Resort Village & Spa **24**
Marriott Village at Lake Buena Vista **17**
Marriott's Orlando World Center **22**
Nickelodeon Family Suites by Holiday Inn **23**
Staybridge Suites Lake Buena Vista **9**

## WALT DISNEY WORLD HOTELS

Disney's All-Star Movies Resort **35**
Disney's All-Star Music Resort **34**
Disney's All-Star Sports Resort **33**
Disney's Animal Kingdom Lodge **32**
Disney's Caribbean Beach Resort **26**
Disney's Coronado Springs Resort **31**
Disney's Fort Wilderness Resort & Campground **7**
Disney's Pop Century Resort **27**
Disney's Port Orleans Resort **25**
Disney's Wilderness Lodge **5**
Shades of Green on Walt Disney World Resort **1**

**OFFICIAL HOTELS**

Best Western Lake Buena Vista Hotel **14**
Buena Vista Palace Resort **21**
DoubleTree Guest Suites **15**
Hilton in the Walt Disney World Resort **19**
Regal Sun Resort **20**
Royal Plaza **16**

To Orlando

535

Exit 68

Blac... Lake

Villa Ave.

Downtown Disney Marketplace

Downtown Disney West Side

Buena Vista Dr.

Typhoon Lagoon

Community Dr.

O'Leans Dr.

Bonnet Creek Pkwy.

Exit 67

Epcot Center Dr.

To: EPCOT, DOWNTOWN DISNEY MARKETPLACE

World Center Dr.

To Kissimmee

To Orlando Int'l Airport

536

Central Florida Greeneway

417

Osceola Pkwy.

To Kissimmee

192

Bonnet Creek

Exit 65

Celebration Pl.

CELEBRATION

To: MAGIC KINGDOM PARK, DISNEY'S HOLLYWOOD STUDIOS, DISNEY'S ANIMAL KINGDOM, DISNEY'S FORT WILDERNESS RESORT & CAMPGROUND

Cayman Way

Sea Breeze Way

Century Dr.

Victory Way

Exit 64

To Tampa

4

International Drive South

DISNEY MARKETPLACE

Epcot Parking

Epcot Transportation Bus

EPCOT

Epcot Resort Blvd.

Epcot Main Entrance/ Toll Plaza

Buena Vista Dr.

Toll Plaza

Guest Parking
Handicap Parking
Bus Transportation

DISNEY'S HOLLYWOOD STUDIOS

Studios Main Entrance/ Toll Plaza

Fantasia Gardens

Winter Summerland

Blizzard Beach

West Buena Vista Dr.

Western Way

Reedy Creek

ESPN WIDE WORLD OF SPORTS COMPLEX

Osceola Pkwy.

World Dr.

192

ANIMAL KINGDOM

To U.S. 27

1/2 mi
0.5 km
0

remote setting. That geyser mentioned above "spouts off" periodically throughout the day just to add to the authenticity, and the nightly electric water pageants can be viewed from the shores of Bay Lake. The lodge also has an immense swimming area, fed by a thundering waterfall whose water flows in from the "hot springs" in the lobby. The nearest park is the Magic Kingdom, but because the resort is in a remote area, it can take some time to get there. The main drawback is the difficulty in accessing other areas via the WDW Transportation System.

901 W. Timberline Dr. (on the southwest shore of Bay Lake just east of the Magic Kingdom; P.O. Box 10000), Lake Buena Vista, FL 32830-1000. ✆ **407/934-7639** or 407/824-3200. Fax 407/824-3232. www.disneyworld.com. 909 units. $240–$815 lodge; $575–$1,455 suite; $330–$1,180 villa. Extra person $25. Children 17 and younger stay free in parent's room. AE, DC, DISC, MC, V. Free self-parking; valet parking $12. **Amenities:** 3 restaurants; 2 lounges; babysitting; bike rentals; concierge; concierge-level rooms; health club & limited spa; 2 Jacuzzis; 2 heated outdoor pool; kids' pool; room service; watersports equipment rentals; WDW Transportation System; transportation to non-Disney parks for a fee. *In room:* A/C, TV, DVD (villa), fridge (villa; free, upon request at the lodge), hair dryer, Internet access (fee), microwave (villa).

## MODERATE

**Disney's Caribbean Beach Resort** ★★ **Value**   Thanks to its moderate pricing scheme and recreational activities, the Caribbean Beach is a great choice for families. The resort's rooms are spread across five villages (all Disney moderate resorts share a similar general layout) of pastel-colored buildings, each named for the islands of Aruba, Barbados, Jamaica, Martinique, and Trinidad (north and south). Try to snag a corner room here if you can, as they let in more light, but don't bother springing for a pool view (those rooms can get noisy). In 2009, 384 rooms in Trinidad South were completely overhauled with a pirate theme, complete with ship-shaped beds and treasure-chest dressers. The closest park is Disney's Hollywood Studios, though it can take up to 45 minutes to get there using Disney transportation—it's best to rent a car if you stay here.

900 Cayman Way (off Buena Vista Dr.; P.O. Box 10000), Lake Buena Vista, FL 32830-1000. ✆ **407/934-7639** or 407/934-3400. Fax 407/934-3288. www.disneyworld.com. 2,112 units. $149–$304 double. Extra person $15. Children

17 and younger stay free in parent's room. AE, DC, DISC, MC, V. Free self-parking. **Amenities:** Restaurant; food court; lounge; babysitting; bike rentals; Jacuzzi; large outdoor heated pool; 6 smaller pools in the villages; kids' pool; room service; watercraft/equipment rentals; WDW Transportation System; transportation to non-Disney parks for a fee. *In room:* A/C, TV, Internet (fee), fridge (free upon request), hair dryer.

### Disney's Coronado Springs Resort ★

An American Southwestern theme carries through four- and five-story grand hacienda–style buildings in desert-sand stucco, with terra-cotta tile roofs and shaded courtyards. The pool area, inspired by the Mayan ruins of Mexico, sports a tremendous Mayan temple with cascading water and a twisting water slide. The rooms are identical in layout to those in the Caribbean Beach Resort, including the small bathrooms. Those located nearest the central public area, pool, and lobby tend to be a bit noisier. Because it's a convention resort, you'll find extras (such as a barber and salon, a variety of suites, and Wi-Fi access for a fee among other perks) not found at Disney's other "moderate" resorts. The nearest park is Animal Kingdom, but the Coronado is at the southwest corner of WDW and a good distance from most other areas in the park; rent a car.

1000 Buena Vista Dr. (near All-Star resorts and Blizzard Beach), Lake Buena Vista, FL 32830. ✆ **407/934-7639** or 407/939-1000. Fax 407/939-1003. www.disneyworld.com. 1,921 units. $154–$269 double; $350–$1,290 suite. Extra person $15. Children 17 and younger stay free in parent's room. AE, DC, DISC, MC, V. Free self-parking. **Amenities:** Restaurant; grill/food court; 2 lounges; bike rentals; concierge; health club & limited spa; Jacuzzi; 4 outdoor heated pools; kids' pool; room service; sauna; watercraft rentals; WDW Transportation System; transportation to non-Disney parks for a fee; limited Wi-Fi (fee). *In room:* A/C, TV, fridge, hair dryer, Wi-Fi (fee).

### Disney's Port Orleans Resort ★★ Value

Port Orleans has the best location, landscaping, and perhaps the coziest atmosphere of the resorts in this class (and was renovated from top to bottom in recent years, so it's in great condition, too). This southern-style property is really a combination of two distinct resorts; the French Quarter and Riverside. The French Quarter offers magnolia trees, wrought iron railings, cobblestone streets, and an idealistic vision of New Orleans's famous French Quarter. Riverside transports you back to Louisiana's Mississippi River towns, its rooms housed in buildings resembling grand plantation homes and the rustic wooden shacks of the bayou. The pools, Tom Sawyer–style playgrounds, and array of activities (including a pirate-themed cruise that departs right from the resort) make it a favorite for families. The rooms and bathrooms (equivalent to all rooms at Disney's moderate resorts) are somewhat of a tight fit for four, though the Alligator Bayou rooms have a trundle bed that allows for an extra child, and the vanity areas have privacy curtains. Port Orleans is just east of Epcot and Disney's Hollywood Studios.

2201 Orleans Dr. (off Bonnet Creek Pkwy.; P.O. Box 10000), Lake Buena Vista, FL 32830-1000. (C) **407/934-7639** or 407/934-5000. Fax 407/934-5353. www. disneyworld.com. 3,056 units. $149–$264 double. Extra person $15. Children 17 and younger stay free in parent's room. AE, DC, DISC, MC, V. Free self-parking. **Amenities:** 2 restaurants; grill/food court; 2 lounges; babysitting; bike rentals; concierge; Jacuzzi; 6 heated outdoor pools; 2 kids' pools; room service; watersports equipment rentals; WDW Transportation System; transportation to non-Disney parks for a fee. *In room:* A/C, TV, fridge, hair dryer, Internet (fee).

### Shades of Green on Walt Disney World Resort ★ (Value)

Shades of Green, nestled among three of Disney's golf courses near the Magic Kingdom, is open only to folks in the military and their spouses, military retirees and widows, 100% disabled veterans, and Medal of Honor recipients. If you qualify, don't think of staying anywhere else—it's the best bargain on WDW soil. A $92-million refit in 2004 doubled the room capacity of the resort and added fully ADA-compliant rooms with wide doorways and roll-in showers. In addition to the added rooms and suites (housing up to eight), existing rooms (among the largest in all of Disney at just over 400 sq. ft.) were completely overhauled. All rooms offer TVs with wireless keyboards (access to the Internet is offered for a fee), balconies or patios, and pool or golf-course views. Transportation—though slow—is available to all of the Disney parks and attractions.

1950 W. Magnolia Dr. (across from the Polynesian Resort). (C) **888/593-2242** or 407/824-3400. Fax 407/824-3665. www.shadesofgreen.org. 587 units. $93–$135 double (based on military rank); $250–$275 6- to 8-person suite (regardless of rank). Extra person $15. Children 17 and younger stay free in parent's room. Cribs $5/night. AE, DC, DISC, MC, V. **Amenities:** 2 restaurants; cafe; 2 lounges; babysitting; concierge; health club; 2 heated outdoor pools; kids' pool; 2 lighted tennis courts; WDW Transportation System; transportation to non-Disney parks for a fee. *In room:* A/C, TV, fridge, hair dryer.

## INEXPENSIVE

The three All-Star Resorts are pretty isolated in WDW's southwest corner. Renting a car is a far better choice than the Disney Transportation System.

**Disney's All-Star Movies Resort**   Most kids love the larger-than-life themes at the three All-Star resorts; however, it can be Disney overload for many adults. Movies such as *Toy Story, 101 Dalmatians,* and *Fantasia* live on in a very big (and I mean BIG) way at this family-friendly resort. They add the only Disney flair to what is essentially a no-frills, budget motel with basic, tiny (only 260 sq. ft.) rooms. Think old-school roadside motels, when all you expected was a clean bed and a bathroom (the ones here are positively Lilliputian). The soundproofing leaves something to be desired, especially with the number of children staying here.

1991 W. Buena Vista Dr., Lake Buena Vista, FL 32830-1000. © **407/934-7639** or 407/939-7000. Fax 407/939-7111. www.disneyworld.com. 1,900 units. $82–$174 double. Extra person $10. Children 17 and younger stay free in parent's room. AE, DC, DISC, MC, V. Free self-parking. **Amenities:** Food court; lounge; babysitting; 2 outdoor heated pools; kids' pool; room service; WDW Transportation System; transportation to non-Disney parks for a fee. *In room:* A/C, TV, Internet (fee), fridge(fee), hair dryer.

**Disney's All-Star Music Resort**   Giant trombones and musical themes from jazz to calypso are the only things differentiating this from the other All-Star resorts (they're all clones of each other—including the microscopic bathrooms—except for the different themes). While the extra frills at the other Disney resorts won't be found at the All-Stars, the rooms do have a significant perk: They're the least expensive (by a large margin) of all the Disney resorts. Most people, however, don't come to WDW to lounge in their rooms, so if you're only going to be here to sleep, the cramped quarters may not be so bad. The closest parks are Blizzard Beach and Animal Kingdom, which you can reach (not necessarily

> **(Tips)  Value in the Eyes of the Beholder**
>
> Disney's All-Star resorts charge a "preferred room" rate, but
> don't expect much for the top rate of $174. Guests who
> book it are paying for location: Preferred rooms are closer
> to the pools, food court, and/or transportation. If you've
> got a rental car or don't mind walking, don't bother paying
> extra; some of the quietest rooms at the All-Stars are the
> standard ones (those farthest from the action).

in an expedient manner) via the Disney Transportation System.
*Tip:* Larger families with smaller budgets can still stay at the
Mouse's house thanks to a recent room redesign at this resort. The
rehab brought with it the addition of larger, more comfortable
family suites.

1801 W. Buena Vista Dr. (at World Dr. and Osceola Pkwy.; P.O. Box 10000), Lake
Buena Vista, FL 32830-1000. (𝒸 **407/934-7639** or 407/939-6000. Fax 407/939-
7222. www.disneyworld.com. 1,920 units. $82–$174 double; $190–$355 suites.
Extra person $10. Children 17 and younger stay free in parent's room. AE, DC,
DISC, MC, V. Free self-parking. **Amenities:** Food court; lounge; babysitting; 2
outdoor heated pools; kids' pool; room service; WDW Transportation System;
transportation to non-Disney parks for a fee. *In room:* A/C, TV, fridge (fee), hair
dryer, Internet (fee).

**Disney's All-Star Sports Resort**   It's an instant replay of the
other All-Star resorts, including the tight quarters (if you aren't a
team player, the togetherness may cause frayed tempers after a
while). The difference here is the theme, with buildings designed
around football, baseball, basketball, tennis, and surfing themes.
The turquoise surf buildings have huge waves along the roofs with
colorful surfboards mounted on exterior walls and pink fish swimming along balcony railings. Again, if your threshold for visual
overload is low, you may want to choose a different resort. As
mentioned above, the rates and themes draw mostly families with
little kids, and the noise level can get quite high.

1701 W. Buena Vista Dr. (at World Dr. and Osceola Pkwy.; P.O. Box 10000), Lake Buena Vista, FL 32830-1000. *(C)* **407/934-7639** or 407/939-5000. Fax 407/939-7333. www.disneyworld.com. 1,920 units. $82–$174 double. Extra person $10. Children 17 and younger stay free in parent's room. AE, DC, DISC, MC, V. Free self-parking. **Amenities:** Food court; lounge; babysitting; 2 outdoor heated pools; kids' pool; room service; WDW Transportation System; transportation to non-Disney parks for a fee. *In room:* A/C, TV, fridge (fee), hair dryer, Internet (fee).

**Disney's Pop Century Resort** (Value) Gigantic memorabilia representing the hottest fads of decades past—from Duncan Yo-Yos and the Rubik's Cube to flower power and 8-tracks—mark the exteriors of the Pop Century's buildings. Another clone of the All-Star school (though a slight step up because the accommodations are relatively newer and the furniture a tad nicer), you won't get a lot of frills, but the price is right for families on a budget. A family of four could, with a bit of effort, squeeze into the small, basic rooms. The resort is closest to the ESPN Wide World of Sports Complex but a bit of a ride from everything else (yes, you should definitely rent a car).

1050 Century Drive Dr. (off the Osceola Pkwy.; P.O. Box 10000), Lake Buena Vista, FL 32830-1000. *(C)* **407/938-4000** or 407/939-6000. Fax 407/938-4040. www.disneyworld.com. 2,880 units. $82–$174 double. Extra person $10. Children 17 and younger stay free in parent's room. AE, DC, DISC, MC, V. Free self-parking. **Amenities:** Food court; lounge; babysitting; 3 heated outdoor pools; kids' pool; room service; WDW Transportation System; transportation to non-Disney parks for a fee. *In room:* A/C, TV, fridge (fee), hair dryer, Internet (fee).

## A DISNEY CAMPGROUND

**Disney's Fort Wilderness Resort & Campground** ★ (Kids) Pines, cypress trees, lakes, and streams surround this woodsy 780-acre resort. The only disadvantage of staying here is the distance from Epcot, Disney's Hollywood Studios, and Animal Kingdom (it is close to Magic Kingdom). But if you're a true outdoors type, you may appreciate the feeling of being more sheltered from some of the Mickey madness. There are 784 campsites for RVs, pull-behind campers, and tents (110/220-volt outlets, grills, and comfort areas with showers and restrooms).

Some sites are open to pets (the ones with full hook-ups)—at an additional cost of $3 per site, not per pet, which is less expensive than using the WDW resort kennel, where you pay $13 to $18 per pet. The 408 wilderness cabins (actually trailers made to look like cabins) offer 504 sq. feet, enough for six people once you pull down the Murphy beds, and they also include kitchens and daily housekeeping service. Cabins also feature an outside deck with grill. Roughing it Disney style isn't so rough with all the comforts of home. In addition, there are plenty of outdoor recreational activities, including horseback riding, fishing, swimming, a petting farm, and playgrounds. The nightly campfire and marshmallow roast, followed by a Disney movie shown right in the great outdoors, is a big hit with families.

3520 N. Fort Wilderness Trail (P.O. Box 10000), Lake Buena Vista, FL 32830-1000. ℂ 407/934-7639 or 407/824-2900. Fax 407/824-3508. www.disneyworld. com. 784 campsites, 408 wilderness cabins. $44–$121 campsite double; $270–$435 wilderness cabin double. Extra person $2 campsites, $5 cabins. Children 17 and younger stay free in parent's room. AE, DC, DISC, MC, V. Free self-parking. Pets $5 (full hook-up sites only), $13–$23 at the on-site kennel. **Amenities:** Restaurant; grill; lounge; dinner show; character dining (seasonal); babysitting; bike rentals; extensive outdoor activities (archery; fishing; horse-back, pony, carriage and hay rides; campfire programs; and more); 2 outdoor heated pools; kids' pool; 2 lighted tennis courts; watersports equipment rentals; WDW Transportation System; transportation to non-Disney parks for a fee. In room (cabins only): A/C, TV/VCR, hair dryer, kitchen, outdoor grill.

# 4 "OFFICIAL" HOTELS IN LAKE BUENA VISTA

These properties, designated "official" Walt Disney World hotels, are located on and around Hotel Plaza Boulevard, which puts them at the northeast corner of WDW. Traffic can be a frustration, as the boulevard is a main access route to Downtown Disney from the outside world.

Guests at these hotels enjoy some WDW privileges (see "The Perks of Staying with Mickey," earlier in this chapter), including free bus service to the parks, but **be sure to ask when booking** which privileges you'll get because they do vary from hotel to hotel.

You can make reservations for all of the below-listed properties through the **CRO** (☎ **407/934-7639**) or through the direct hotel numbers included in the listings. To ensure you get the best rates, however, call the hotel or its parent chain directly to see if there are special rates or packages available.

## EXPENSIVE

**Buena Vista Palace Resort** ★★   The most upscale of the Hotel Plaza Boulevard–area properties, popular with business and leisure travelers alike (though business people make up 75% of its guests) now sports a chic and trendy new look. Guest rooms have an eclectic mix of stylishly hip furnishings and a trendy color scheme of white, aqua, and brown (unfortunately comfort, most notably in the living area, has been sacrificed for appearance's sake—the bedding, however, is quite cozy). Many of the upscale business-standard rooms, in addition to upgraded amenities, have balconies or patios; ask for one above the fifth floor with a "water view." That's the side facing the pools on Recreation Island, Downtown Disney, and, in the distance, Disney's Hollywood Studios' Tower of Terror. The "Disney view" offers distant views of Epcot's IllumiNations fireworks but little else. Families will appreciate the Island Suites, with over 800 sq. feet of space, one and a half baths, a microwave, fridge, and proximity to the pools and playgrounds. You'll find the best rates are offered in July and August, contrary to the mainstream tourist resorts—a bonus due to its popularity with the business set.

1900 Buena Vista Dr. (just north of Hotel Plaza Blvd.; P.O. Box 22206), Lake Buena Vista, FL 32830. ☎ **866/397-6516** or 407/827-3228. Fax 407/827-6034. www.buenavistapalace.com or www.downtowndisneyhotels.com. 1,012 units. $89–$239 double; $219–$1,520 suite. $13 daily resort fee. Extra person $20. Children 17 and younger stay free in parent's room. AE, DC, DISC, MC, V. Self-parking free; valet parking $16. **Amenities:** 2 restaurants; grill; 2 lounges; character breakfast on Sun; babysitting; concierge; concierge-level rooms; health club; Jacuzzi; 3 heated outdoor pools; kids' pool; room service; sauna; spa; lighted tennis court; complimentary bus service to WDW parks; transportation to non-Disney parks for a fee. *In room:* A/C, TV, fridge, hair dryer, minibar, microwave (suite), Wi-Fi (fee).

**Best Western Lake Buena Vista Hotel** ★ Value · This 12-acre lakefront hotel is reasonably modern, with nicer rooms and public areas than you might find in others within the chain. Rooms are located in an 18-story tower, and all have balconies. The views improve from the eighth floor and up, and those on the west side have a better chance of seeing something Disney. Accommodations in this category are usually a step above the "moderates" inside WDW, and this one is not an exception. You can reserve an oversize room (about 20% larger) or a WDW fireworks–view room for a few dollars more a night. *Note:* It definitely pays to surf the corporate website **www.bestwestern.com** if you plan to stay here. It sometimes offers great deals and special rates for this hotel.

2000 Hotel Plaza Blvd. (btw. Buena Vista Dr. and Apopka–Vineland Rd./Hwy. 535), Lake Buena Vista, FL 32830. ✆ **800/348-3765** or 407/828-2424. Fax 407/828-8933. www.lakebuenavistaresorthotel.com. 325 units. $89–$239 standard for 4; $299–$439 suite. Resort fee $9. 5th person $15. AE, DC, DISC, MC, V. Free self-parking; valet parking $10. **Amenities:** Restaurant; cafe; lounge; babysitting; concierge; fitness center; outdoor heated pool; kids' pool; room service; tennis courts; Wi-Fi (free); complimentary bus service to WDW parks; transportation to non-Disney parks for a fee. *In room:* A/C, TV, fridge (fee, available upon request), game system (fee), hair dryer, Wi-Fi (free).

**DoubleTree Guest Suites** ★★ Children have their own check-in desk and theater, and they get a gift upon arrival at this hotel, the best of the "official" hotels for families (how can you not love a hotel that gives you freshly baked chocolate chip cookies at check-in?). All of the accommodations in this seven-story hotel are two-room suites that offer 643 sq. feet—large by most standards—with space for up to six; none have balconies, but some have patios. This is the easternmost of the "official" resorts, which means it's farthest from the Disney action, but closest to (even within walking distance of) the shops, restaurants, and activities located in the Crossroads Shopping Center, or along Apopka–Vineland Road.

2305 Hotel Plaza Blvd. (just west of Hwy. 535/Apopka–Vineland Rd.), Lake Buena Vista, FL 32830. ✆ **800/222-8733** or 407/934-1000. Fax 407/934-1011. www.downtowndisneyhotels.com or www.doubletreeguestsuites.com. 229 units. $140–$290 double. Extra person $20. Children 17 and younger stay free in parent's room. AE, DC, DISC, MC, V. Free self-parking. **Amenities:** Restaurant; 2 lounges; babysitting; concierge; health club; heated outdoor pool; kids' pool; limited room service; 2 lighted tennis courts; complimentary bus service to WDW parks; transportation to non-Disney parks for a fee. *In room:* A/C, 2 TVs, fridge, game system (fee), hair dryer, Internet, microwave.

**Hilton in the Walt Disney World Resort** ★★★ This upscale resort welcomes many a Disney vacationer, even though business travelers constitute the bulk of its clientele. Its major claim to fame: It's the only official resort on Hotel Plaza Boulevard to offer guests Disney's Extra Magic Hour option (see p. 130 for details). The recently renovated rooms have an upscale and contemporary Shaker-style decor, as well as upgraded amenities, and they offer plenty of space; Junior Suites are the best choice for families. Rooms on the north and west sides of floors 6 though 10 offer a view of Downtown Disney (just a short walk away) and, in the distance, the Magic Kingdom fireworks. The resort has a large pool area (with two pools and plenty of space to soak up the sun) and a game room for kids.

1751 Hotel Plaza Blvd., Lake Buena Vista, FL 32830. (C) **407/827-4000.** Fax 407/827-6369. www.hilton.com. 814 units. $199–$339 double; $359–$1,500 suite. Extra person $20. Children 17 and younger stay free in parent's room. AE, DC, DISC, MC, V. Self-parking $8; valet parking $15. **Amenities:** 4 restaurants; 2 cafes; 3 lounges; character breakfast (Sun); babysitting; concierge;

---

 **Tips** **Excess Charges**

Several of the properties in this chapter add daily resort fees to their room rates. Though it's essentially a legal version of price gouging, charging for services that used to be included in the rates, such as use of the pool, admission to the health club, or in-room coffee or phones has become a growing trend. Be sure to ask when you make your reservations to see if your hotel charges such a fee and, if so, exactly what's included (some may even be optional) so you're not blindsided at checkout.

---

concierge-level rooms; health club; 2 outdoor heated pools; room service; complimentary bus service to WDW parks; transportation to non-Disney parks for a fee. *In room:* TV, fridge (fee), hair dryer, Internet (fee), microwave (fee), minibar, MP3 docking station, Wi-Fi (fee).

**Regal Sun Resort** ★ The guest rooms at this recently renovated lakeside resort now sport updated furnishings, cozy bedding, upgraded amenities (such as flatscreen TVs), and a stylish decor. Other notable changes include the addition of a new zero-entry pool and aquatic playground, a children's lounge (with scheduled activities), and a completely redesigned lobby. Its frequent package deals make it popular with budget travelers. Ask for a Tower Room on the west side (floors 9–19) for a limited view of Lake Buena Vista. A Saturday night MurderWatch Mystery Theatre dinner show ($50 adults, $15 kids 3–9) is held in the LakeView restaurant for an entertaining evening away from Disney. A character breakfast is also offered 3 mornings a week.

1850 Hotel Plaza Blvd. (just east of Buena Vista Dr.), Lake Buena Vista, FL 32830. ✆ **800/624-4109** or 407/828-4444. Fax 407/828-8192. www.regalsunresort. com. 626 units. $65–$199 double. $10 daily resort fee. Extra person $20. Children 17 and younger stay free in parent's room. AE, DC, DISC, MC, V. Free self-parking; valet parking $10. **Amenities:** Restaurant; 3 lounges; character breakfast (Tues, Thurs, Sat); babysitting; children's activity program; concierge; health club; Jacuzzi; 2 outdoor heated pools; 2 lighted tennis courts; complimentary bus service to WDW parks; transportation to non-Disney parks for a fee. *In room:* A/C, TV, fridge, MP3 docking station, Wi-Fi (fee).

**Royal Plaza** ★ A favorite with the budget-minded, the Hotel Royal Plaza's hallmark is a friendly staff who provide excellent service. The well-sized rooms sport quality furnishings and amenities (pull-out sofas, plasma TVs, and more) and have enough space for five. Poolside rooms have balconies and patios; the tower rooms have separate sitting areas, and some offer whirlpool tubs in the bathrooms. If you want a view from up high, ask for a room facing west and WDW; the south and east sides keep a watchful eye on I-4 traffic. The inner courtyard offers a quiet escape where you can sit by the pool and soak up the Florida sunshine surrounded by scattered palm trees.

1905 Hotel Plaza Blvd. (btw. Buena Vista Dr. and Hwy. 535/Apopka–Vineland Rd.), Lake Buena Vista, FL 32830. ✆ **800/248-7890** or 407/828-2828. Fax 407/827-6338. www.downtowndisneyhotels.com or www.royalplaza.com. 394 units. $129–$199 double; $189–$269 suite. $8 daily resort fee. Children 17 and younger stay free in parent's room. AE, DC, DISC, MC, V. Self-parking $8; valet parking $16. **Amenities:** Restaurant; lounge; Kids Eat Free program; babysitting; children's activity program; health club; heated outdoor pool; room service; 4 lighted tennis courts; complimentary bus service to WDW parks; transportation to non-Disney parks for a fee. *In room:* A/C, TV, game system, hair dryer, Internet (fee), minibar.

# 5 OTHER LAKE BUENA VISTA AREA HOTELS

The hotels in this section are within a few minutes' drive of the WDW parks. They offer a great location but not the Disney-related privileges given to guests in the "official" hotels, such as Disney bus service and character breakfasts. On the flip side, because you're not paying for those privileges, hotels in this category are generally a shade less expensive for comparable rooms and services.

## EXPENSIVE

**Marriott's Orlando World Center ★★★**   This is an upscale resort that caters to both business and leisure travelers alike. Golf, tennis, and spa lovers will find plenty to do at this 230-acre resort. The large, comfortable, and beautifully decorated rooms sleep four, and the higher poolside floors offer views of Disney. For a large-scale resort, it is surprisingly easy to get around, as it is not so much spread out as up. The largest of its five pools has water slides and waterfalls surrounded by plenty of space to relax among the palm trees and tropical plants. The location, only 2 miles from the Disney parks, is a fabulous plus. Special offers (in the past, these have included getting a second room or an early booking bonus at a substantial savings) and vacation packages (often associated with

**Marriott Montage**

The December 2000 christening of **Marriott Village at Lake Buena Vista,** 8623 Vineland Ave., Orlando, FL 32821 (© **877/682-8552** or 407/938-9001; www.orlando 2stay.com), brought together three of the flagship's properties in a cluster just east of Lake Buena Vista, 3 miles from WDW. The resort includes a 400-room Spring-Hill Suites ($169–$189 double; free continental breakfast), a 388-room Fairfield Inn ($159–$179 double; free continental breakfast), and a 312-room Courtyard by Marriott ($169–$189 double). Children 17 and under stay free in their parents' rooms, and an extra person costs an additional $10.

Wi-Fi is available at all three resorts for an additional fee (in-room at the Fairfield; in the public areas at the Courtyard and Springhill Suites) and all rooms have free high-speed Internet access, a PlayStation, and fridges (the SpringHill Suites also has microwaves, and the Fairfield features 48 bunk-bed suites for families). Each resort has its own pool and play area (the Courtyard features an indoor/outdoor pool with an interactive splash zone for the kids), though guests may use whichever pool they choose. The fitness center, Hertz rental-car desk (located at the Courtyard), arcade, and Marketplace are also shared. All offer transportation for a fee ($5–$15 per person per day) to Disney parks and non-Disney parks. There are three restaurants within walking distance, as well as an array of on-the-go and snack-style eateries located right in the village itself.

area theme parks, most notably SeaWorld) are offered throughout the year (including plenty of extra perks), making the resort more affordable than you might otherwise think.

8701 World Center Dr. (on Hwy. 536 between I-4 and Hwy. 535/Apopka–Vineland Rd.), Orlando, FL 32821. ℂ **800/621-0638** or 407/239-4200. Fax 407/238-8777. www.marriott.com. 2,111 units. $349–$409 for up to 5; $750–$1,600 suite. Children 17 and younger stay free in parent's room. AE, DC, DISC, MC, V. Self-parking $13; valet parking $23. **Amenities:** 4 restaurants; food court; 2 lounges; babysitting; concierge; concierge-level rooms; golf course (nearby); health club; 3 heated outdoor pools; heated indoor pool; kids' pool; room service; sauna; spa; 8 lighted tennis courts; transportation to all theme parks for a fee; limited Wi-Fi (fee). *In room:* A/C, TV, game system (fee), hair dryer, Internet (fee), minibar, MP3 docking station.

## MODERATE

### Embassy Suites Lake Buena Vista ★

Set near the end of Palm Parkway, just off Apopka–Vineland Road, this fun and welcoming all-suite resort remains a quiet retreat. Each suite sleeps five and includes a separate living area (with a pullout sofa) and sleeping quarters. The roomy accommodations and on-site activities (including "dive"-in movies 4 nights a week) make it a great choice for families. Some of the other perks here include a complimentary cooked-to-order breakfast, a nightly manager's reception, free transportation to Disney, and an indoor/outdoor pool.

8100 Lake Avenue, Orlando, FL 32836. ℂ **800/362-2779** or 407/239-1144. Fax 407/239-1718. www.embassysuiteslbv.com. 334 units. $99–$270 suite, extra person $15. Rates include full breakfast, manager's reception. AE, DC, DISC, MC, V. Free self-parking; valet parking $12. **Amenities:** Restaurant; cafe; lounge; babysitting; concierge; health club; indoor and outdoor heated pools; kids' pool; room service; sauna; tennis court; free shuttle to Disney parks. *In room:* A/C, TV, fridge, hair dryer, kitchenette, microwave, Wi-Fi (fee).

### Hawthorn Suites Lake Buena Vista ★

These moderately priced family suites are less than 2 miles from Disney. This hotel is a good choice if you want a little home-style comfort and the chance to perform do-it-yourself stuff in the fully equipped kitchen. The two-bedroom suites sleep up to eight and offer plenty of room to rest and relax. A complimentary buffet breakfast, free Wi-Fi, and evening receptions are just some of the perks you'll enjoy when staying here. Special offers and packages can often save you a few more dollars, rewarding you for longer stays; some include tickets to Disney.

8303 Palm Pkwy. (off S. Apopka–Vineland Rd./Hwy. 535), Orlando, FL 32836. ✆ 866/756-3778 or 407/597-5000. Fax 407/597-6000. www.hawthornlake buenavista.com. 120 units. $89–$169 double. Extra person $15. Rates include continental breakfast. Children 18 and younger stay free in parent's room. AE, DC, DISC, MC, V. Free self-parking. **Amenities:** Health club; Jacuzzi; outdoor heated pool; free shuttle to Disney parks; transportation to non-Disney parks for a fee. *In room:* A/C, TV, hair dryer, fully equipped/stocked kitchen, microwave, Wi-Fi (free).

### Holiday Inn SunSpree Resort Lake Buena Vista ★ Kids

Just a mile from the Disney parks, this spruced-up inn caters to kids in a big way. They can check in at their own check-in desk (they'll even get a free goodie bag), watch a movie at the theater in the lobby area, or have fun at the arcade. The hotel's 231 Kid Suites have beds for up to six and themes (an igloo, a space capsule, castle, and more); however, standard rooms (with separate kitchenettes) are also available. If you like sleeping in, ask for a room that doesn't face the pool area. Kids younger than 12 eat free in their own restaurant, though fine dining it isn't (kids won't care about that anyway). The resort also offers plenty of other dining options.

13351 Apopka–Vineland Rd./Hwy. 535 (btw. Hwy. 536 and I-4), Lake Buena Vista, FL 32821. ✆ 800/366-6299 or 407/239-4500. Fax 407/239-7713. www. hisunspreelbv.com or www.holidayinn.com. 507 units. $99–$159 standard for up to 4; $119–$179 Kid Suite. AE, DISC, MC, V. $5.95 resort fee. Free self-parking. Pets less than 30 pounds $40 for a 7-night stay, 2-pet maximum. **Amenities:** Restaurant; food court; Kids Eat Free program; babysitting; supervised children's program; health club; Jacuzzi; outdoor heated pool; kids' pool; room service; free shuttle to Disney parks; transportation to non-Disney parks for a fee. *In room:* A/C, TV, fridge, game system (fee), hair dryer, kitchenette, microwave, Wi-Fi (fee).

### Lake Buena Vista Resort Village & Spa ★★★

Near the southern end of International Drive, within walking distance of the **Lake Buena Vista Factory Stores,** this relatively new ownership-based resort offers spacious two-, three-, and four-bedroom apartment-style accommodations ranging in size from 1,080 square feet to 2,170 square feet, each tastefully decorated in tropical Tommy Bahama–style furnishings. Fully stocked full-size kitchens appointed with granite countertops and rich dark wood cabinetry, washers and dryers, plasma televisions, and master suites with Jacuzzis are the norm here. Kids and adults alike will love the 7,500-square-foot zero-entry lagoon-style, pirate-themed pool (with a waterslide that winds its way through a 70-foot-long life-size pirate ship equipped with shooting water cannons). Swaying hammocks are scattered about the surrounding sundeck while cabanas allow for a poolside massage. You can grab a bite to eat or sip on tropical concoctions poolside—a large entertainment deck provides a view of the entire pool. For those seeking a more relaxing experience, the full-service Reflections Spa offers a tranquil undersea-inspired atmosphere with a slew of services guaranteed to rejuvenate even the most weary traveler. Its location—just off World Center Drive—allows for quick access to almost all the parks: Disney is less than 5 minutes by car and SeaWorld (Discovery Cove and Aquatica) is just a bit farther (about 10 min.), though Universal is more removed (approx. 20 min.-plus from the resort). Complimentary shuttle service is available to all of the major theme parks.

8113 Resort Village Dr. (off S. Apopka Vineland Rd./Hwy.535), Lake Buena Vista, FL 32821-1000. ✆ **866/401-2699** or 407/597-0214. Fax 407/597-1600. www. lbvorlandoresort.com. 498 units. $129–$499. Extra person $25. Children 17 and younger stay free in parent's room. AE, DC, DISC, MC, V. Self-parking free. **Amenities:** Restaurant; cafe; grill; 2 lounges; babysitting; supervised children's program; concierge; health club; Jacuzzi; 2 outdoor heated pools; children's water play area; room service; spa; transportation to all major theme parks at no charge. *In room:* A/C, multiple TVs, hair dryer, Internet (free), fully equipped and stocked full-size kitchen; washer and dryer.

**Nickelodeon Family Suites by Holiday Inn** ★★ (Kids) This is one of the best properties in the Orlando area for families. Its two-bedroom Kid Suites feature a second bedroom for the kids with bunk or twin beds, kitchenettes, and a pullout sofa in the living area. Three-bedroom suites are also available and include additional space, a second bathroom, a full kitchen, upgraded amenities, and a trendy decor. The resort's two pool areas (with lots of lifeguards) are veritable water parks, with extensive multilevel water slides, flumes, climbing nets, and water jets. Activities are scheduled poolside (including Slime Time), and there is also a wide variety of recreational options, including a small minigolf course, playgrounds, and sand play areas. "Nick After Dark," an evening supervised activity program for kids ages 5 to 12, allows parents to take a night off. A daily character breakfast is offered in addition to the hotel's regular breakfast buffet (at the latter, kids eat free with paying adults). The only downside is that the resort's incredible popularity translates to an incredibly crowded, often overwhelming experience—combine this with a day at the theme parks and parents may be in need of a vacation from their vacation. Discounted rates are available for stays on off-peak nights and at select times throughout the year.

14500 Continental Gateway (off Hwy. 536), Lake Buena Vista, FL 32821. ℭ **877/642-5111,** 407/387-5437, or 866/NICK-KID (642-5543). Fax 407/387-1489. www.nickhotel.com. 777 units. $130–$552 suite. AE, DC, DISC, MC, V. Free self-parking. **Amenities:** Restaurant; food court; lounge; supervised children's program; extensive children's activities; 2 Jacuzzis; 2 water-park pools; free shuttle to Disney and non-Disney parks. *In room:* A/C, TV, fridge, game system, hair dryer, Internet (free), full kitchen (select suites), microwave.

**Staybridge Suites Lake Buena Vista** ★★   This chain hotel is ideally located close to the action of the theme parks, as well as area restaurants and shops. Spacious rooms, reasonable pricing, and a friendly staff make this an excellent choice for families. Featured are one- and two-bedroom suites (which sleep up to eight), all with full kitchens; two-bedroom suites have two full bathrooms. The suites have large, comfortable separate living areas when compared to other all-suite hotels. Stocking up on necessary supplies, snacks, and assorted sundries is much less of a hassle because a full-service grocer is located next door.

8751 Suiteside Dr., Orlando, FL 32836. ℭ **800/866-4549** or 407/238-0777. Fax 407/238-2640. www.sborlando.com. 150 units. $109–$179. Rates include full breakfast. Rollaway beds and cribs available at no charge. AE, DC, DISC, MC, V. **Amenities:** 24-hr. exercise room; Jacuzzi; outdoor heated pool; children's pool; free shuttle to Disney parks. *In room:* A/C, TV/VCR, hair dryer, free high-speed Internet access, kitchen.

## INEXPENSIVE

**Hampton Inn Orlando/Lake Buena Vista**   Location rules at this modern property, which is only 1 mile from the entrance to Hotel Plaza Boulevard on the northeast corner of Disney. It's not fancy, but it's clean and comfortable, the price is right, and the perks include a free full hot breakfast (at the hotel or on the go—packed in a grab-and-go bag for when you're in a hurry to get to the parks) and free high-speed Internet. Nearby are plenty of places to eat and shop.

8150 Palm Pkwy., Orlando, FL 32836. ℂ **800/370-9259** or 407/465-8150. Fax 407/465-0150. www.orlandolakebuenavista.hamptoninn.com. 147 units. $89–$129 for up to 4. Extra person $10. Rates include a continental breakfast. Children 17 and younger stay free in parent's room. AE, DC, DISC, MC, V. Free self-parking. **Amenities:** Concierge; exercise room; Jacuzzi; outdoor heated pool; free shuttle to Disney parks; transportation to non-Disney parks for a fee. *In room:* A/C, TV, fridge (select rooms), hair dryer, microwave (select rooms), Wi-Fi (free).

# Where to Dine

It should come as no surprise that Orlando has something for everybody when it comes to pleasing the palate, ranging from fast food to five-star restaurants and everything in between. The city overflows with more than 5,000 dining options, though it's usually noted for its many theme and chain restaurants. Though the local dining scene doesn't compare to that found in such metropolitan foodie hot spots as New York, San Francisco, or Las Vegas, there are certainly more than a few places here that could easily hold their own against the competition. That said, Orlando is the undisputed king of U.S. family destinations, and restaurants generally do their darnedest to cater to their target audience.

*Note to parents:* Keep in mind that most moderate to inexpensive restaurants have kids' menus ($5–$9), and many offer distractions, such as coloring books and crayons, in the hopes it will keep your little ones otherwise occupied until their dinner arrives. If you go to a place catering to children, expect the noise level to be high. Parents in need of a night off from the kids can arrange for in-room babysitting or supervised child care (p. 189) so they too can indulge in one of the area's finer dining options.

For additional online information about area restaurants, visit **www.orlandoinfo.com**, **www.go2orlando.com**, or the websites in the listings that follow.

The restaurants outside of the parks can all be found on the "Walt Disney World & Lake Buena Vista Accommodations & Dining" map on p. 52.

## ADVANCE RESERVATIONS AT WDW RESTAURANTS

Walt Disney World's Advance Reservations system, while similar to a reservation, is not nearly as rigid. Essentially, the system guarantees that you will get the next available table that will accommodate your party *after* you've arrived at a restaurant (which should be 5–10 min. prior to the time you've reserved). In other words, a table isn't kept empty while the restaurant waits for you. As such, it's likely that you'll end up waiting anywhere from 15 to 30 minutes, even if you arrive at the time you scheduled your meal. You can arrange Advance Reservations 180 days in advance at most full-service restaurants in the Magic Kingdom, Epcot, Disney's Hollywood Studios, Animal Kingdom, and Disney resorts. Advance Reservations can also be made for character meals (p. 95) and dinner shows throughout the World. To make arrangements, call ✆ **407/939-3463;** groups of eight or more can also call ✆ **407/939-7707.** In mid-2009, Disney also started taking advance reservations online through the **disneyworld.com** website.

Nighttime dinner-theater shows (p. ˙96) can be booked up to 180 days in advance as well. Be aware, however, that these dinner shows require full payment in advance and that cancellations must be made at least 48 hours prior to the time of the show to avoid penalties. ***Note:*** Since the Advance Reservations phone number was instituted in 1994, it has become much more difficult to obtain a table as a walk-in for the resorts' more popular restaurants. I *strongly* advise you to call as far ahead as possible, especially if you're traveling during the peak seasons. Amazingly, some restaurants, especially the dinner shows and character meals, can book up quite literally within only a minute or two of the phone lines opening (7am EST) on that 180th day out.

If you don't make your dining plans in advance, you can take your chances by making your Advance Reservations once you have arrived in the parks. In addition to the places listed below, you can always head directly to your desired restaurant to see what's available.

- **In Epcot** at Guest Relations on the East side of Spaceship Earth.
- **In the Magic Kingdom** via the telephones at several locations including the Walt Disney World Railroad station just inside the entrance, and at City Hall near the front of Main Street U.S.A.
- **In Disney's Hollywood Studios** via the telephones just inside the entrance or at Guest Relations near Hollywood Junction.

- **In Animal Kingdom** at Guest Relations on the left near the entrance. (Note that Rainforest Cafe here is a *verrry* popular place, so the sooner you call for Advance Reservations, the better.)

Also, keep these restaurant facts in mind:

- All Florida restaurants and bars that serve food are **smoke free.**
- The Magic Kingdom (including its restaurants) serves no alcoholic beverages, but liquor is available at Animal Kingdom, Epcot, and Disney's Hollywood Studios restaurants and elsewhere in the WDW complex.
- All sit-down restaurants in Walt Disney World take American Express, Diners Club, Discover, MasterCard, Visa, and the Disney Visa Card.
- Unless otherwise noted, restaurants in the parks **require park admission.**
- Guests staying at Disney resorts and official properties can make restaurant reservations through Guest Services or the concierge.
- Nearly all WDW restaurants with sit-down or counter service offer children's menus with items ranging from $5 to $9, though in a few cases they're $10 to $12. Some include beverages and sides.

## 1 THE BEST DINING BETS

- **Best for Kids:** Kids adore the meals served up with Disney characters bounding about, and there are plenty to choose from throughout the **Walt Disney World** resorts and theme parks. (For the scoop, see "Dining with Disney Characters," p. 95.) They also love the eclectic atmosphere, sounds, and visuals of the jungle-themed **Rainforest Cafe** at Downtown Disney Marketplace (© **407/827-8500**) and Animal Kingdom (© **407/938-9100**). Monkey business is strongly encouraged there. If horsing around is more your style, try dining at the **Whispering Canyon Café** (© **407/939-3463**) inside Disney's Wilderness Lodge for some foot-stomping fun.

- **Best Character Meal:** It doesn't get any better than **Chef Mickey's** breakfasts and dinners at the Contemporary Resort (© 407/939-3463). These "events" have their respective namesake and other characters, but a word of warning: They also attract *up to 1,600 guests* each morning. A close second is a meal at the **Crystal Palace Buffet** (© 407/939-3463), located in the Magic Kingdom. You will not see Mickey and Minnie, but your kids will be greeted at your table by Winnie the Pooh, Tigger, and some of their pals.
- **Best View:** The **California Grill** (© 407/939-3463), high atop Disney's Contemporary Resort, offers a spectacular view of the Magic Kingdom, as well as a front-row seat for the park's nightly fireworks display through its immense floor-to-ceiling windows.
- **Best Outdoor Dining:** The terrace at **Artist Point** (© 407/939-3463), the premier restaurant at Disney's Wilderness Lodge, overlooks a lake, waterfall, and scenery evocative of America's national parks. The **Rose & Crown Pub & Dining Room** at Epcot (© 407/939-3463) delivers a front-row seat for the IllumiNations fireworks display.

## 2 WHERE TO DINE IN WALT DISNEY WORLD

From fast food on the fly to fine-dining establishments, there are literally hundreds of restaurants scattered throughout Walt Disney World, including those at the theme parks, the Disney resorts, and the "official" hotels. Portions are generally large, practically ensuring that you'll never walk away hungry, though prices match portion sizes accordingly. Be prepared to spend a rather hefty amount each day for just a few meals, a snack, and a drink (or two).

To help you out a bit, the restaurants in this chapter have been categorized by **the price of an average entree** per person. In this chapter, restaurants in the Inexpensive category charge less than $10 for an entree; those in the Moderate category charge anywhere from $11 to $20. Expensive restaurants will set you back $21 to

$30, and do note that when you toss in drinks, appetizers, side dishes, desserts, and the tip, the final tally at even a moderate restaurant can get rather high. Be sure to budget accordingly.

*One last note:* The restaurants I list in this chapter occasionally change menus (sometimes seasonally, occasionally weekly, in some cases even daily). So items I feature here may not necessarily be on the menu when you visit. And, as entrees vary, so do prices.

# IN THE MAGIC KINGDOM
## Expensive

**Cinderella's Royal Table** ★ AMERICAN    You'll be greeted by handmaidens before making your way inside this royal restaurant—by far the most popular place to dine in the Magic Kingdom. Those who enter are usually swept off their feet as they're transported back to a time when medieval kings and queens reigned (a feeling that's helped along by the Gothic interior, which includes leaded-glass windows, stone floors, and high-beamed ceilings). The servers treat you like a lord or lady (I'm not kidding; that's how they'll address you) and the menu has fetching names, but the fine print reveals traditional entrees. Pan-seared salmon, braised lamb, and roasted prime rib are just a sampling of the choices.

*Note:* Because of its location and ambience, a meal here is sought by everyone from little girls who dream of Prince Charming to romantics seeking a more intimate meal. The problem: This is actually one of the smallest dining rooms in the World, making Advance Reservations a must. And you'll have your work cut out for you to get one—it may very well take several calls (and a lot of flexibility on your part) to ensure a spot.

Cinderella Castle, Fantasyland. ℂ **407/939-3463.** www.disneyworld.com. Advance Reservations recommended. Character breakfast adult $47, child $31; character lunch adult $51, child $32; character dinner adult $57, child $35. AE, DC, DISC, MC, V. Daily 8–11:15am, noon–3pm, and 4pm–1 hr. before park closing.

**Tony's Town Square Restaurant** ITALIAN    Inspired by the cafe in *Lady and the Tramp,* Tony's dishes up lunches and dinners of pastas and pizzas in a pleasant if somewhat harried dining room featuring etched glass and ornate gingerbread trim. The lunch

**Tips** **Special Tastes**

When it comes to eating at Disney, just because something's not on the menu doesn't mean it's not available. Looking for kosher food? Worried WDW can't entertain your vegetarian taste buds? What about low sodium, low sugar, or fat-free diets? Disney can usually handle these and other lifestyle diets as well as other special dietary requirements (meals for those with allergies or lactose intolerance) at any of their full-service restaurants as long as guests give advance notice—3 days is suggested to accommodate special dietary needs, while at least 24 hours is necessary for lifestyle diets (48 hr. if you are dining at the WDW Swan & Dolphin, Yak & Yeti, Rainforest Cafe, or T-Rex). This holds true for other dining requests, too. If you are headed to one of the resort's restaurants and know your kids may have a tough time with the menu, chicken nuggets and some other kid-friendly items can be requested in advance. It's easiest to make special requests when you make your Advance Reservations (☎ **407/939-3463**), or, if you're staying at a Disney resort, by stopping by the lobby concierge desk.

menu includes sandwiches, salads, and pizzas, along with such entrees as pasta primavera, spaghetti and meatballs, and the catch of the day. Evening fare might include chicken Florentine, seafood in a spicy tomato sauce, or a New York strip steak. Kids will enjoy the pizzas and plainer pastas. Original cels from the movie (including the film's famous spaghetti smooch) line the walls. *Tip:* Dinner is by far the busiest time to dine here, but if you time it just right, you can see the Wishes fireworks display after your meal while remaining close enough to the park exit to make a quicker getaway than most.

Main St. © **407/939-3463**. www.disneyworld.com. Main courses $12–$17 lunch, $17–$28 dinner. AE, DC, DISC, MC, V Daily 11:30am–3pm, and 5pm–park closing.

## Moderate

**Liberty Tree Tavern** AMERICAN   Step into a replica of an 18th-century Colonial pub and its historic atmosphere, including oak-plank floors and a big brick fireplace hung with copper pots. Lunch includes seafood (such as cured salmon and crab cakes), sandwiches, salads, soups, burgers, roast turkey, and pot roast. The nightly dinner is a set family-style meal (now sans characters) that includes salad, roast turkey, carved beef, smoked pork loin, with mashed-potatoes, stuffing, and macaroni and cheese—along with cherry cobbler and vanilla ice cream to top it off.

Liberty Sq. © **407/939-3463**. www.disneyworld.com. Advance Reservations. Main courses $12–$18 lunch; dinner adult $31, child $15. AE, DC, DISC, MC, V. Daily 11:30am–3pm and 4pm–park closing.

## Inexpensive

**Columbia Harbour House** ★AMERICAN/SEAFOOD   This small restaurant often goes overlooked because of its size, but it does offer some rather decent light fare. Battered fish and shrimp; hummus; tuna sandwiches; a harvest salad with chicken, veggies, cheese, and sunflower seeds; vegetarian chili; clam chowder; and fruit are featured on the menu.

Liberty Sq. © **407/939-3643**. www.disneyworld.com. Advance Reservations not accepted. All items $7–$9. AE, DC, DISC, MC, V. Daily 11am–park closing.

**Cosmic Ray's Starlight Café** AMERICAN   The largest of the park's fast-food spots, this cafe features an appropriately huge menu. Three separate counters, similar to a food court, serve a variety of chicken options (whole- or half-rotisserie, dark meat, white meat, fried or grilled), ribs, sandwiches, burgers, hot dogs, veggie wraps, soups, and salads. The combination of its casual atmosphere and varied menu makes Ray's a great choice for those with kids (who also enjoy the occasional mealtime entertainment by "alien" Sonny Eclipse). Do note, however, that you may have to wait in more than one line here, as each station offers a different

## On Again, off Again . . . on Again

The menu at **Tomorrowland Terrace Noodle Station** includes chicken and beef dishes, egg rolls, and other Asian-themed cuisine along with chicken nuggets and a wide selection of kids' meals. It's one of the prettiest and largest outdoor seating areas in the park; you can eat out in the fresh air even as you get a respite from the hot Florida sun. As an added bonus, you get a great view of the gardens, waterways, and Cinderella Castle. If you've picked up a sweet treat along one of Main Street's eateries and can't find a place to sit down (often the case), this is the perfect place to head, as it's often overlooked by visitors. *Note:* The Noodle Station is a seasonal eatery that's open sporadically, so be sure to check your guide map to see if it's open when you're visiting. All items cost $7 to $9.

Another on-again/off-again eatery at the Magic Kingdom is the **Diamond Horseshoe.** This saloon-themed space functions as a counter-service dining spot only when the park is in need of an additional spot for guests to dine. Check your *Times Guide* to see if it's open when you're visiting—in the past, it has served up sandwiches during lunch and full-fledged dinners during the holidays and peak travel seasons. Because it's not well publicized, it's often a quieter and less-crowded option than the usual hot spots.

WHERE TO DINE

5

WHERE TO DINE IN WDW

selection. Other minuses: The large dining area fills up quickly at lunch and dinner, and the noise level is generally high. *Tip:* Kosher meals are available here for direct-purchase (though they're pricey and not particularly noteworthy in the taste department).

Main St. ☏ **407/939-3463.** www.disneyworld.com. Advance Reservations not accepted. All items $7–$14. AE, DC, DISC, MC, V. Daily 11am–park closing.

**Pecos Bill Café** ★ AMERICAN  Set in an old-time saloon of sorts, with ornate wrought iron accents, tile work scattered throughout, heavy flamelike chandeliers, and a golden stucco interior, this sit-and-go fast-food joint serves up burgers, hot dogs, salads, a barbecue pork sandwich, and a great chicken wrap sandwich. Its good location—just between Frontierland and Adventureland—means that those traveling clockwise through the park will probably hit the area just in time for lunch.

*Tip:* If your cravings run more toward Mexican than American, head through the indoor seating area in the back to the seasonal **El Pirata y Perico,** a covered outdoor snack spot featuring tacos, empanadas, chips, and taco salad (most less than $8).

Frontierland. ✆ **407/939-3643.** www.disneyworld.com. Advance Reservations not accepted. All items $7–$9. AE, DC, DISC, MC, V Daily 11am–park closing.

**Plaza Restaurant** AMERICAN   It shouldn't be confused with the nearby Plaza Ice Cream Parlor, but the sundaes, banana splits, and other ice-cream creations at this popular dining spot are arguably the best in WDW. This 19th-century inspired restaurant features tasty if expensive sandwiches (turkey, Reuben, cheesesteak, chicken, vegetarian, tuna, and burgers) that come with an order of fries or potato salad.

Main St. ✆ **407/939-3463.** www.disneyworld.com. Advance Reservations recommended. Meals $10–$13; ice cream $4.50–$7. AE, DC, DISC, MC, V Daily 11am–park closing.

## AT DISNEY'S HOLLYWOOD STUDIOS

Some of the most uniquely themed restaurants in all of WDW are set among the movie sets, action-packed shows, and wild rides of Disney's Hollywood studios. That fact, in turn, makes them some of the most difficult to get into. Be sure to make Advance Reservations if you want to eat at any full-service restaurant here. Listed below are the best of the bunch.

### Expensive

**Hollywood Brown Derby** AMERICAN   This elegant restaurant is modeled after the famed Los Angeles celebrity haunt where Louella Parsons and Hedda Hopper once held court. It features some of the finest food and the fanciest surroundings in the park—along with some of the highest prices. White linens top dark wood tables, chandeliers and amber lighting set the mood, and potted palms all add to the upscale atmosphere. More than 1,500 caricatures of its most famous patrons through the years line the walls, including those of Lucille Ball, Bette Davis, and Clark Gable. Owner Bob Cobb created the original restaurant's signature Cobb salad in the 1930s. (It's so popular that this Derby serves more than 31,000 of them a year.) Dinner entrees at Disney's version include pan-fried grouper with balsamic roasted asparagus; sesame-seared Ahi tuna with honey-gingered spaghetti squash, shitake broth, and Wasabi oil; and roasted pork rib chop with smoked cheese tomato fondue. The Derby's signature dessert, grapefruit cake with cream-cheese icing, is the perfect way to end your meal.

Hollywood Blvd. ☎ **407/939-3463.** www.disneyworld.com. Advance Reservations recommended. Main courses $23–$35 lunch and dinner; Fantasmic! package varies (a la carte pricing). AE, DC, DISC, MC, V Daily 11:30am–park closing.

## Moderate

**50's Prime Time Café** (Kids) AMERICAN   Several homey dining rooms at this cafe, separated by knickknack-lined shelves and curtained windows, look just like Mom's kitchen did back in the 1950s, complete with Formica countertops, a stove, fridge, and black-and-white TVs showing clips from classics such as *My Little Margie*. The servers add to the fun, greeting diners with such lines as, "Hi Sis, I'll go tell Mom you're home," and they may threaten to withhold dessert if you don't eat all your food or catch you with your elbows on the table. Kids love it. The entrees—fried chicken, meatloaf (ask for extra catsup), pot roast, and open-faced sandwiches, among others—aren't quite as good as Mom used to make, but are decent nonetheless. The desserts, viewed via a View-Master, include s'mores, sundaes, and cakes; they're all definitely worth the wait. Beer and a varied list of specialty drinks (they make a mean margarita) are served. Kids will get a kick out of the glowing *electric* ice cubes in their drinks.

Near the Indiana Jones Stunt Spectacular. ☎ **407/939-3463.** www.disney world.com. Advance Reservations recommended. Main courses $12–$17 lunch, $13–$21 dinner. AE, DC, DISC, MC, V Daily 11am–park closing.

## Epcot Dining

Though dining at one of the World Showcase pavilions is a traditional part of the Epcot experience, many of the following establishments are rather overpriced when compared to an equivalent restaurant beyond the park's boundaries. Try eating lunch at the full-service restaurants when the price for a meal is much lower.

**Advance Reservations** are strongly recommended for sit-down restaurants. Otherwise, the chances of getting a table without a wait—often a long wait—are pretty slim. Call ✆ **407/939-3463** for Advance Reservations.

**Expensive**    For seafood, you can't beat **Coral Reef** (Living Seas Pavilion; main courses $13–$28 lunch, $21–$31 dinner; daily 11:30am–3pm and 4:30pm–park closing). The dining room surrounds a 5.6-million-gallon aquarium filled with tropical fish and a coral reef.

The hand-set mosaic tiles, latticed shutters, and painted ceiling at **Marrakesh** ★ (Morocco Pavilion; main courses $15–$22 lunch, $21–$28 dinner, $28–$43 prix fixe; daily noon–park closing) exemplifies the spirit of Epcot more than any other restaurant. The menu features marinated beef and chicken shish kabobs.

**Moderate**    The **Biergarten** (Germany Pavilion; lunch buffet adult $20, child $11; dinner buffet adult $33, child $14; daily noon–3:45pm and 4pm–park closing) has an all-you-can-eat Bavarian buffet of assorted sausages, pork schnitzel, sauerbraten, spaetzle, and sauerkraut.

**Mama Melrose's Ristorante Italiano** ITALIAN    Found along the "movie" set of a New York street, this large, casual neighborhood eatery welcomes diners with red checkered table cloths, wood floors, and red vinyl booths. The best bets here are the wood-fired

If you're in the mood for steak, **Le Cellier Steakhouse** (Canadian Pavilion; main courses $14–$31 lunch, $20–$37 dinner; daily noon–3pm and 3:30pm–park closing) is the right place; offerings include the usual range of cuts. The lunch menu features lighter fare, including sandwiches and salads.

Visitors from the U.K. flock to **Rose & Crown Pub & Dining Room** (United Kingdom Pavilion; main courses $11–$15 lunch, $15–$25 dinner; daily 11am–1 hr. before park closes) for cod and chips wrapped in newspaper, bangers and mash, and warm bread pudding. If you only want to grab a pint or a snack at the bar, you don't need Advance Reservations.

At **San Angel** ★ (Mexico Pavilion; main courses $17–$25 lunch, $17–$33 dinner; daily 11:30am–park closing), you can dine under starry skies (a la Disney) and feast on some of the best south-of-the-border cuisine in all of the theme parks.

**Inexpensive** For counter service, check out **La Cantina de San Angel** (Mexico Pavilion; meals $8–$9; daily 11am–4 hr. before park closes) for a decent burrito, taco, or churro.

The grab-and-go options at **Kringla Bakeri og Kafe** (Norway Pavilion; sandwiches and salads $4–$10, treats $2–$6; daily 11am–park closing) include a smoked salmon and scrambled eggs, and smoked ham and Jarlsberg cheese sandwiches, and an array of tempting pastries.

flatbreads (grilled pepperoni, four-cheese, vine-ripened tomato, and others) offered at both lunch and dinner. The dinner menu also includes seafood in a spicy marinara sauce and oak-grilled salmon.

Near the Backlot Tour. **407/939-3463.** www.disneyworld.com. Advance Reservations recommended. Main courses $13–$20 lunch, $12–$22 dinner, Fantasmic! dinner package $33 adult, $12 children. AE, DC, DISC, MC, V. Daily noon–park closing.

**Sci-Fi Dine-In Theater Restaurant** (Kids) AMERICAN  This restaurant's simulated nighttime sky is filled with fiber-optic twinkling stars that look down on you as you sit in a chrome "convertible" watching a giant screen showing '50s and '60s sci-fi flicks, zany newsreels, cartoons, and B horror-movie clips. The menu includes a selection of sandwiches, ribs, burgers, seafood, pasta, steak, and salads. Drinks are served with souvenir glow-in-the-dark ice cubes. The food is average; it's the atmosphere that keeps the crowds coming.

Near Indiana Jones Epic Stunt Spectacular. © **407/939-3463.** www.disney world.com. Advance Reservations recommended. Main courses $12–$23 lunch or dinner. AE, DC, DISC, MC, V Daily 11am–park closing.

### Inexpensive
**Toy Story Pizza Planet** AMERICAN  The menu here is far from original, but it will satisfy some of the younger (and pickier) eaters in your family with pizza, salad, drinks, and desserts. It's a big favorite of kids, thanks to the array of arcade games located just next door—just remember to bring plenty of change.

In the Muppet's Courtyard. © **407/939-3463.** www.disneyworld.com. Advance Reservations not accepted. All meals $6–$9 AE, DC, DISC, MC, V. Daily 11am–park closing.

## IN THE ANIMAL KINGDOM
### Moderate
**Rainforest Cafe** ★ (Kids) CALIFORNIA  Expect California fare with an island spin at this Rainforest. Menu offerings tend to be tasty and somewhat creative, with far more choices than most can contend with. Fun dishes include Mogambo Shrimp (sautéed in olive oil and served with penne pasta), Rumble in the Jungle Turkey Wrap (with romaine, tomatoes, and bacon), and Maya's Mixed Grill (ribs, chicken breast, and shrimp). Tables situated among the

**Tips** **It All Adds Up**

If you plan on taking in one of Disney's many popular character-dining experiences or dinner shows, plan on paying a bit extra if you find yourself dining during the holidays. Disney's added an extra $5 (or so) to the price of their character meals and dinner shows during select times throughout the year (including, but not limited to, the days and sometimes weeks surrounding New Year's, Easter, Memorial Day, July 4th, Labor Day, Thanksgiving, and the Christmas holidays). For details (including the exact dates that Disney's holiday pricing is in effect), check out **www.disneyworld. com** or call ✆ **407/939-3463.**

dining room's dense vines and generally inanimate animals are usually packed; that's partially due to the lack of other full-service dining options at Animal Kingdom, but also due to the actual popularity of this loud (thanks in part to the cracks of thunder and chatter of animals) and lively establishment.

Just outside Animal Kingdom entrance. *Park admission not required* (though there is an entrance from inside the park, too). ✆ 407/938-9100. www.rain forestcafe.com. Advance Reservations strongly recommended. Main courses $9–$14 breakfast, $13–$32 (most less than $25) lunch and dinner. AE, DC, DISC, MC, V. Daily 8:30am–6 or 7pm. Parking $14.

**Yak & Yeti** ★ ASIAN FUSION/PACIFIC RIM This Pan-Asian restaurant offers both sit-down and counter-service dining in a uniquely eclectic and meticulously detailed setting that blends seamlessly into the Himalayan village surrounding it. The menu's specialties include crispy wok-fried green beans (even the kids will love these); lettuce cups filled with minced chicken, chopped veggies, and a yummy maple tamarind sauce; seared miso salmon; crispy mahimahi; and maple tamarind chicken. Be sure to leave room for dessert—the mango pie and fried wontons (filled with cream cheese and served with skewers of fresh pineapple, vanilla ice cream, and a sweet honey vanilla drizzle) are simply delish. Kids will appreciate the miniburgers, veggie lo mein, egg rolls, and chicken bites. An outdoor counter-service outpost (offering many, but not all, of the items from the main restaurant menu) is located just to the right of the entrance—it makes a great alternative for those who prefer to dine outdoors in the villagelike setting.

In Asia, near Expedition Everest. ☎ **407/939-3463.** www.disneyworld.com. Advance Reservations suggested. Lunch and dinner $16–$25, kids 3–9 $8–$11. AE, DC, DISC, MC, V Daily 11am–park closing.

### Inexpensive

**Tusker House** AFRICAN/AMERICAN   The thatched-roof Tusker House in Harambe village now features a buffet with a definite culinary flair. Several stations, each with a different selection of African-inspired items, are located throughout the inviting open-air market-style interior. Blatjang chutneys with South African preserves, sambals tabbouleh, hummus and baba ghanouj, curried rice salad, couscous with roasted vegetables, vegetable samosas, seafood stew, roasted chicken, and a variety of other offerings are all on the menu. Kids will find a selection of familiar favorites (including PB&J, chicken drumsticks, mac 'n' cheese, and corn-dog nuggets, among others) to please their pint-sized palate. A character breakfast (Donald's Safari Breakfast) is offered in the morning. A slightly shaded stone patio out back with a view over the trees allows you to relax and enjoy your meal tucked away from the crowds. Out front, the pavilion offers shade, and if timed right a view of the live entertainment.

In Africa, near entrance. ☎ **407/939-3463.** www.disneyworld.com. Advance Reservations suggested for breakfast. Breakfast $21 adult, $12 kids 3–9; lunch $21 adult, $12 kids; dinner $29 adult, $14 kids. AE, DC, DISC, MC, V Daily 8–10:30am, 11:30am–3:30 or 4pm, and 4–6pm.

## IN THE WALT DISNEY WORLD RESORTS

Most restaurants listed in this category continue the Disney trend of being above market price. On the flip side, many offer food and atmospheres that far exceed what you'll find in the theme parks. The quality level means that even those not staying at Disney resorts like to dine at these restaurants, so Advance Reservations are a must if you don't want to miss out on a table.

## Expensive

**Artist Point** ★★ (Finds) SEAFOOD/STEAKS/CHOPS    Enjoy a grand view of Disney's Wilderness Lodge and tasty cuisine at this rustically elegant establishment. Immense windows overlook the waterfalls, rocky landscaping, and the resort's own Fire Rock geyser. The menu changes seasonally and might feature grilled buffalo sirloin with sweet potato hazelnut gratin and sweet onion jam, but the restaurant's signature is the cedar plank–roasted king salmon with asparagus, haricot vert, mizuna, herb dumplings, and sage brown-butter vinaigrette. Expect a reasonably extensive wine list that now exclusively features wines from the Pacific Northwest.

901 W. Timberline Dr., in Disney's Wilderness Lodge. ℂ **407/939-3463.** www. disneyworld.com. Advance Reservations recommended. Dinner $25–$45, wine pairing $28. AE, DC, DISC, MC, V Daily 5:30–10pm. Free self- and valet parking.

**Boma** ★★★ (Moments) AFRICAN    Here's a truly unique and worthwhile dining experience. This restaurant's warm and welcoming atmosphere, evoking an African marketplace, is enhanced by

---

### (Tips) For Smaller Stomachs

If your kids aren't satisfied with the offerings on the kids' menu (though many feature pint-size portions of more adult options along with plenty of familiar favorites), try the appetizer menu. They'll have more to choose from, and the price is right. Also, always ask if half-portions are available; they are generally not advertised, though some restaurants offer them upon request. The same applies when requesting items a la carte. Disney's menus (even at quick service restaurants) won't always reflect a la carte items, though they are often available if you ask.

colorful banners strewn from high above. An authentic thatched roof and large wooden tabletops made from tremendous tree trunks add to the impressive decor. In front of the open exhibition kitchen is an incredible buffet of international cuisine featuring authentic dishes from more than 50 African nations. Adventurous diners can expect such treats as Moroccan seafood salad (mussels, scallops, shrimp, and couscous), curried coconut seafood stew, chicken pepper pot soup, and much more. The watermelon rind salad is a specialty and is both delicious and refreshing—just don't forget to save room for the yummy desserts. Kids with less sophisticated taste buds can dine on traditional American favorites. There's also a breakfast buffet (try the specialty juices—they're delicious).

2901 Osceola Pkwy., at Disney's Animal Kingdom Lodge. ℂ **407/939-3463.** www.disneyworld.com. Advance Reservations recommended. Breakfast buffet $19 adults, $11 kids 3–9; dinner buffet $31 adults, $15 kids. AE, DC, DISC, MC, V Daily 7–11am and 5–10pm. Valet or free self-parking.

**California Grill** ★★★ CALIFORNIA  Located on the Contemporary Resort's 15th floor, this stunning restaurant offers views of the Magic Kingdom and lagoon below while your eyes and mouth feast on an eclectic menu. A Wolfgang Puckish interior incorporates Art Deco elements (curved pearwood walls, vivid splashes of color, polished black granite surfaces) with a charged and upbeat atmosphere, but the central focus is an exhibition kitchen with a wood-burning oven and rotisserie. The menu's headliners change to take advantage of fresh market fare but may include pan-roasted Atlantic salmon with fingerling potatoes, edamame, and orange soy butter; and oak-fired filet of beef with Gruyere-potato pave, broccoli, and teriyaki barbecue sauce. The Grill also has a nice sushi and sashimi menu (tuna, crab, and shrimp, among others) ranging from appetizers to large platters. This is one of the few spots in WDW that isn't inundated with kids. The list of California wines helps complement the meal and views.

*Note:* It can be tough to get a table at the Grill, especially on weekends and during Disney fireworks hours, so make a reservation as early as possible. Also be aware that a business casual dress code is required.

4600 N. World Dr., at Disney's Contemporary Resort. ☎ **407/939-3463.** www. disneyworld.com. Advance Reservations required and need a credit card guarantee. Main courses $28–$44; sushi and sashimi $21–$28. AE, DC, DISC, MC, V Daily 5:30–10pm. Valet or free self-parking.

**Flying Fish Café** ★ SEAFOOD   Chefs at this upscale Coney Island–inspired restaurant take the stage in a show kitchen that turns out entrees such as potato-wrapped red snapper with a creamy leek fondue and red wine butter sauce-pan seared Ahi tuna with Moroccan couscous. The food is better than what you'll find at the **Coral Reef** (p. 82) and **Cape May Café** (p. 92), but not quite in the same league as **Todd English's bluezoo** (p. 90). Vibrantly colored tile floors, lily pads, and golden fish, along with delicate jellyfish-like lighting, hanging by fish hooks from high above, and accents of shimmering fish scales combine to create an undersea ambience. *Note:* If you can't get a table here, ask to sit at the counter—you'll get a great view of the exhibition kitchen.

2101 N. Epcot Resorts Blvd., at Disney's BoardWalk. ☎ **407/939-3463.** www. disneyworld.com. Advance Reservations recommended. Main courses $28–$42. AE, DC, DISC, MC, V. Daily 5:30–10pm. Valet or free self-parking.

**Jiko—The Cooking Place** ★★ AFRICAN   The Animal Kingdom Lodge's signature restaurant offers a nice diversion from

---

### ⓘ Tips   A Balancing Act

In an effort to promote better eating habits, Disney kids' menus have been revised; children's entrees now feature healthy options such as low-fat milk, 100% fruit juice, water, and such sides as unsweetened applesauce, veggies, and fresh fruit as standard items. Soda pop and french fries are still available, but only upon request.

All the WDW restaurants (in the theme parks and at the resorts) are currently in the midst of transitioning to become entirely trans fat–free (a trend that is also taking hold at other area theme parks).

Disney's more conventional offerings and a complementary addition to the multicultural dining rooms at Epcot's World Showcase. Jiko's show kitchen, sporting two wood-burning ovens, turns out an innovative and creative menu of international cuisine with African overtones. Dishes, depending on the season, might include Durban shrimp curry, broiled filet of Arctic char with braised beetroots and roasted potatoes; or wood-grilled filet mignon. An impressive wine list features South African vintages exclusively.

2901 Osceola Pkwy., at Disney's Animal Kingdom Lodge. ℂ **407/939-3463.** www.disneyworld.com. Advance Reservations recommended. Main courses $26–$41 AE, DC, DISC, MC, V. Daily 5:30–10pm. Valet or free self-parking.

**Kouzzinas** MEDITERRANEAN Replacing Spoodles is Kouzzinas, run by celebrity Iron Chef Cat Cora. While changes to the restaurant's decor have been minimal—the show kitchen remains intact, albeit in updated form—the menu is now filled with authentic family recipes with a Mediterranean flavor. Simple yet creative dishes might include cinnamon stewed chicken, chargrilled lamb burgers, or fishermen's stew, with sides ranging from smashed garlic fried potatoes to chilled salt-roasted beets. The pizza window is popular—you can pick up a slice ($3.50–$4) or order an entire pie to go (starting at $18).

2101 N. Epcot Resorts Blvd., at Disney's BoardWalk. ℂ **407/939-3463.** www.disneyworld.com. Reservations recommended. Main courses $16–$28. AE, DC, DISC, MC, V. Daily 5:30-10pm. Pizza Window 5pm–midnight. Valet or free self-parking.

**Todd English's bluezoo** ★★★ SEAFOOD Set inside the WDW Dolphin, this is the hippest, hottest, most happening place

---

**Fun Facts** **Hidden Mickey?**

All over the Walt Disney World Resort, you'll find Mickey Mouse popping up in some rather interesting places. You better take a good look at your food before you take a bite; you may be surprised to find it staring back at you.

> ## (Tips) The Whispering Canyon Café
>
> If you're looking for family-oriented dining at the Wilderness Lodge, try the **Whispering Canyon Café,** where a decor dedicated to cowboys and Indians is warm and welcoming. Kids can horse-race on broomsticks, and everyone gets a whoopin' and a hollerin' at dinner. Meals are served family style (though a la carte service is available if you so desire). They're open for breakfast, lunch, and dinner. Entrees run from $12 to $18 at lunch (the buffet is $18), $19 to $29 at dinner (the buffet is $27).

to dine in town. Internationally acclaimed chef Todd English has created an amazing menu of fresh seafood and coastal dishes that are served with creative flair in an artsy undersea setting. An exhibition kitchen showcases the chefs at work. Appetizers include the amazing "Olive's" classico flatbread, a roasted beet salad, and teppan-seared sea scallops. Melt-in-your-mouth entrees include Cantonese lobster, miso-glazed Chilean sea bass, seared nori wrapped tuna, wild salmon block, and roasted swordfish. Unlike the portions at many upscale restaurants of this caliber, those served here are meal-worthy, not minuscule. That said, the prices are hefty and do not include side dishes (veggies, for example), which will run you an extra $7 to $11. Dress is casual (this is Disney), though the atmosphere is definitely adult and upscale.

1500 Epcot Resort Blvd., at the WDW Dolphin. (*C*) **407/934-1111.** www.disney world.com. Advance Reservations highly recommended. Main courses $27–$60. AE, DC, DISC, MC, V. Daily 3:30–11pm. Free self- and validated valet parking (validate ticket on your way out).

## Moderate

**Boatwright's Dining Hall** (**Kids** NEW ORLEANS    A family atmosphere (noisy), good food (by Disney standards), and reasonable prices (ditto) make Boatwright's a hit with Port Orleans Resort guests, if not outsiders. The jambalaya is sans seafood, but is filled with vegetables, rice, chicken, and sausage—all rather spicy and giving it quite a kick. Other dinner items include grilled salmon, slow-roasted prime rib, penne pasta with shrimp, and pot roast. Boatwright's is modeled after a 19th-century boat factory, complete with the wooden hull of a Louisiana fishing boat suspended from its lofty beamed ceiling. Most kids like the wooden toolboxes on every table; each contains a saltshaker that doubles as a level, a wood-clamp sugar dispenser, a pepper-grinder-cum-ruler, a jar of unmatched utensils, shop rags (to be used as napkins), and a little metal pail of crayons. *Note:* Breakfast is no longer being served.

2201 Orleans Dr., in Disney's Port Orleans Resort. (*C*) **407/939-3463.** www. disneyworld.com. Advance Reservations recommended. Main courses $17–$26 dinner. AE, DC, DISC, MC, V. Daily 5–10pm. Free self-parking.

**Cape May Café** SEAFOOD/STEAKS/CHOPS This New England–style clambake offers a selection of oysters, clams, mussels, baked fish, and small peel-and-eat shrimp. Accompaniments include corn on the cob, potatoes, and other assorted veggies. Landlubbers fear not; there is a selection of not-so-fishy fare including barbecued pork ribs and prime rib. The casual nautical theme carries into the restaurant from the surrounding Beach Club resort.

1800 Epcot Resorts Blvd., at Disney's Beach Club Resort. (*C*) **407/939-3463.** www.disneyworld.com. Advance Reservations recommended. Character breakfast $19 adults, $11 children 3–9; dinner buffet $27 adults, $13 children 3–9. AE, DC, DISC, MC, V. Daily 7:30–11am, 5:30–9:30pm. Free self- and valet parking.

**ESPN Club** ★ AMERICAN If you are a sports enthusiast, this is *the* place for you. Sports memorabilia hangs from every wall and television monitors (all 71 of them) surround you at every turn—ensuring you won't miss a minute of the big game. The all-American fare includes such choices as "Boo-Yeah" chili, hot wings, and burgers. Sandwiches and salads are available as well. The service is impeccable—never have I had a waiter so quick on his feet. While the food is quite good, it's the upbeat action-packed atmosphere that draws the crowds here.

2101 N. Epcot Resorts Blvd., at Disney's BoardWalk. ☎ **407/939-1177.** www. disneyworld.com. Reservations not needed. $10–$21 lunch and dinner. AE, DC, DISC, MC, V. Mon–Thurs 11:30am–1am; Fri–Sat 11:30am–2am. Valet or free self-parking.

**'Ohana** ★ **Kids** PACIFIC RIM   Its star is earned on the fun front, but the decibel level here can get a bit overwhelming, especially for those looking for a relaxing evening out. Inside, you're welcomed as a "cousin," which fits because *'Ohana* means "family" in Hawaiian. As your food is being prepared over an 18-foot fire pit, the staff keeps your eyes and ears filled with all sorts of shenanigans. The blowing of a conch shell summons a storyteller, coconut races get underway in the center aisle, and you can shed your inhibitions and shake it in the hula lessons. When it starts, the meal is served rapid fire (ask your waiter to slow the pace if it's too fast). The edibles include a variety of skewers (think shish kabob), including turkey, steak, and pork. Trimmings include assorted veggies, potatoes, fried wontons, salad, shrimp, and chicken wings all served up family style. A full bar offers limited wine selections (tropical alcoholic drinks are available for an added fee). ***Note:*** Ask for a seat in the main dining room, or you won't get a good view of the entertainment.

1600 Seven Seas Dr., at Disney's Polynesian Resort. ☎ **407/939-3463.** www. disneyworld.com. Advance Reservations strongly recommended. $25 adults, $14 children 3–9; character breakfast $31 adults, $15 kids 3–9 (p. 99). AE, DC, DISC, MC, V. Daily 7:30–11am and 5–10pm. Free self- and valet parking.

## 3  WHERE TO DINE IN LAKE BUENA VISTA

### EXPENSIVE

**Hemingway's** ★ SEAFOOD   The interior of Hemingway's has an upscale Key West air, and the walls are hung with sepia photos of the author and his fishing trophies. The restaurant has a romantic indoor dining room lit by hurricane lamps, and the wooden deck overlooks a waterfall. Menu highlights include beer-battered coconut shrimp with horseradish sauce and orange marmalade, the lobster crusted sea bass, or the blackened mahimahi with Cajun tartar sauce. The wine list is decent, but to stay in the spirit of the experience order the *Papa Dobles,* a potent rum concoction invented by Hemingway, who, according to legend, once downed 16 at one sitting! It's usually pretty child-free here, though there is a kids' menu.

1 Grand Cypress Blvd., in the Hyatt Regency Grand Cypress Resort. (℗ **407/239-3854.** www.hyattgrandcypress.com. Reservations recommended. Main courses $25–$42. AE, DC, DISC, MC, V. Daily 6–10pm. Free self- and validated valet parking. Take I-4 exit 68, Hwy. 535/Apopka–Vineland Rd., north to Winter Garden–Vineland Rd./Hwy. 535, and then left.

**Mikado Japanese Steakhouse ★★** JAPANESE This restaurant offers a tastier meal and a more intimate atmosphere than the other Japanese steakhouses in the area. The sushi menu is one of the area's best, as is its *teppanyaki.* Here the chefs slice, dice, and send the occasional piece of chicken, seafood, and beef from their grill to your plate, and the chef's addition of a few extra special spices make it the best *teppanyaki* in the area. Shoji screens lend intimacy to a dining area where windows overlook rock gardens, reflecting pools, and a palm-fringed pond.

8701 World Center Dr. (off Hwy. 536), in Marriott's Orlando World Center. (℗ **407/239-4200.** Reservations recommended. Main courses $29–$48. AE, DC, DISC, MC, V. Daily 6–10pm. Free self- and validated valet parking. Take I-4 exit 67/Hwy. 536 east to the Marriott World Center.

## MODERATE

**The Crab House** SEAFOOD Even if it is a chain, this casual restaurant offers a good variety of seafood (and a handful of options for landlubbers) at satisfactory prices. The all-you-can-eat seafood and salad bar is great for those who like variety and has lots of tasty dishes. The regular menu features a variety of fish dishes, seafood, Maine lobster, and, of course, crabs—from Alaskan and king to Maryland blue. *Note:* The chain has several other branches in Orlando.

8496 Palm Pkwy., Orlando, FL. 32836 (just off Apopka–Vineland across and up from Hotel Plaza Blvd.). (℗ **407/239-1888.** www.crabhouseseafood.com. Reservations accepted. Lunch $9–$24, dinner $14–$36; lobster varies according to

exit 68 (Hwy. 535/Apopka–Vineland), turn right, follow past the Crossroads to Palm Pkwy., turn right. The restaurant is back a bit on the right.

## INEXPENSIVE

**Romano's Macaroni Grill** (Value NORTHERN ITALIAN Though it's part of a chain, Romano's has the down-to-earth cheerfulness of a mom-and-pop joint. The menu offers thin-crust pizzas made in a wood-burning oven and topped with such items as barbecued chicken. The grilled chicken portobello (simmering between smoked mozzarella and spinach orzo pasta) alone is worth a visit. Equally good is an entree of grilled salmon with a teriyaki glaze, also with spinach orzo pasta.

12148 Apopka–Vineland Rd. (just north of Hwy. 535/Palm Pkwy.). ℂ **407/239-6676.** www.macaronigrill.com. Main courses $7–$16 lunch, $12–$26 dinner (most less than $20). AE, DC, DISC, MC, V. Sun–Thurs 11am–10pm; Fri–Sat 11am–11pm. Free self-parking. Take I-4 exit 68, Hwy. 535/Apopka–Vineland Rd. north and continue straight when Hwy. 535 goes to the right. Romano's is about 2 blocks on the left.

---

# 4 DINING WITH DISNEY CHARACTERS

---

Dining with your favorite costumed characters is a treat for many Disney fans, but it's a truly special occasion for those younger than 10. Some of the most beloved movie characters seemingly come to life: shaking hands, hugging, signing autographs, and posing for family photos (most never speak, with the exception of the princesses and a very small handful of others), so forget about conversation). These are huge events—it's not uncommon for Chef Mickey's, listed below, to have **1,600 or more guests on a weekend morning**—so make your Advance Reservations as far in advance as possible (when you book your room, if not earlier).

To make reservations for WDW character meals, call ℂ **407/939-3463.**

**Tips**    **Dinner Theater**

The Polynesian Resort's delightful 2-hour **Disney's Spirit of Aloha Dinner Show** (*(©* **407/939-3463;** reservations required; adults $59.99, $54.99, and $50.99, kids 3–9 $30.99, $26.99, and $25.99, including tax and tip; free parking) is like a big neighborhood party. It features Tahitian, Samoan, Hawaiian, and Polynesian singers, drummers, and dancers who entertain you while you feast on a menu that includes tropical appetizers, lanai roasted chicken, Polynesian wild rice, South Seas vegetables, dessert, wine, beer, and other beverages. It all takes place 5 nights a week in an open-air theater (dress for nighttime weather and bring sweaters) with candlelit tables, red-flame lanterns, and tapa paintings on the walls. Reservations should be made 60 days in advance (but can be made up to 180 days in advance—full payment is expected when booking), especially during peak periods such as summer and holidays. Seating is priced in tiers: The closer you sit to the stage, the higher the price you'll pay. Show times are 5:15 and 8pm Tuesday through Saturday. **Note:** Not all the seats for this one are equal, so paying for a better seat is the way to go—but I must warn that the resulting price is really too high for the value received from the production as a whole.

You'll find all of the restaurants mentioned in this section on the map, "Walt Disney World & Lake Buena Vista Accommodations & Dining," p. 52. **Note:** Although the character appearances below were accurate when this book went to press, lineups and booking requirements change frequently (as do menus and prices). If you have your heart set on meeting a certain character, confirm his or her appearance when making your Advance Reservations.

The **Hoop-Dee-Doo Musical Revue** ★★★, at Fort Wilderness Resort & Campground, p. 59 (© **407/939-3463;** reservations required; adults $59.99, $54.99, and $50.99; kids 3-9 $30.99, $26.99, and $25.99 including tax and tip; free parking), is Disney's most popular show, so make reservations *early.* You feast on a down-home, all-you-can-eat barbecue (fried chicken, smoked ribs, salad, corn on the cob, baked beans, bread, salad, strawberry shortcake—all of it quite good, by the way—and your choice of coffee, tea, beer, wine, sangria, or soda). Performers in 1890s garb lead you in a foot-stomping, hand-clapping, high-energy show that includes a lot of jokes you haven't heard since second grade. Reservations should be made at least 180 days in advance (at which time full payment is expected), especially during peak periods such as summer and holidays. Show times are 5, 7:15, and 9:30pm daily (the show lasts about 2 hr.).

The tiered pricing system means that the closer you are to the action, the higher the price you'll pay to enjoy it. For this show, since there's not a bad seat in the house, don't feel the need to splurge.

Here is a list of the current character meals:

- The **Akershus Royal Banquet Hall** (Norway Pavilion, Epcot; character breakfast adult $29, child $18; character lunch adult $36, child $22; character dinner adult $41, child $22; daily 8:30–10am, 11:40am–3pm, and 4:20–8:30pm), set inside a re-created 14th-century castle, now features **Princess Storybook** character meals for breakfast, lunch, and dinner. An impressive smorgasbord including baked salmon with spicy mustard, poached cod, braised lamb and cabbage, and venison stew are among the choices at lunch and dinner. Kids can choose from more familiar options such as grilled chicken, salmon, pasta, hot dogs, pizza, pasta, and turkey sandwiches. The biggest draws are the Disney princesses (excluding Cinderella) that make their way around the hall, stopping at each table to say hello. The popular Princess Story Book Dining (see below) where Snow White, Jasmine, Ariel, Pocahontas, Belle, or Mary Poppins might show up, features American fare.

- The **Cape May Café** (p. 92; $19 adults, $11 children; daily 7:30–11am) serves lavish buffet American breakfasts hosted by Admiral Goofy and his crew—Chip 'n' Dale and Pluto (characters may vary).

- The whimsical **Chef Mickey's** ★★ (4600 N. World Dr., at Disney's Contemporary Resort; breakfast $27 adults, $14 children; dinner $34 adults, $17 children; daily 7–11:30am and 5–9:30pm) offers buffet breakfasts and dinners (entrees change daily; salad bar, soups, vegetables, ice cream with toppings). Mickey and Minnie and various pals make their way to every table while meeting and mingling with guests. While this is one of the largest restaurants offering character dining, if you plan on dining here during spring break and around the holidays, it's best to make Advance Reservations.

- **Cinderella's Royal Table** ★ (p. 76; breakfast $47 adults, $31 children; lunch $51 adults, $32 children; dinner $57 adults, $35 children; daily 8–10:20am, noon–3pm, and 4pm–park closing) serves character breakfast buffets daily, and recently began serving a character fixed menu lunch and dinner as well. Princess hosts vary, but Cinderella always puts in an appearance and the Fairy Godmother joins the celebration for dinner. This is one of the most popular character meals in the park and the hardest to get into, so **reserve far, far in advance** (reservations are taken 180 days in advance, and you must pay in full at the time you make your reservations). To have the best shot at getting in, be flexible about your seating arrangements and dining times, and call Disney exactly at 7am EST on your first date of reservations eligibility (if you aren't sure what date that is, call Disney and they'll help you figure it out). If you get through on your first try (lucky you!), tell the reservations clerk you want Cinderella's Table for whatever date you've picked. Don't even think about requesting a specific time—take whatever you can get (most reservations will be gone by 7:15am).

- Winnie the Pooh and pals hold court at **Crystal Palace Buffet** ★ (at Crystal Palace, in the Magic Kingdom; breakfast $21 adults, $12 children; lunch $23 adults, $13 children; dinner $33 adults, $16 children; daily 8–10:30am, 11:30am–3pm, and 4pm–park closing). The restaurant serves breakfast (eggs, French toast, pancakes, bacon, and more), lunch, and dinner. The latter features a long menu including some type of poultry, beef, seafood, an array of veggies, salads, and kid-friendly favorites.

- At **Donald's Safari Breakfast** ★, Donald, Goofy, and Pluto host a safari-themed buffet breakfast (eggs, bacon, French toast, and more) in Africa's **Tusker House** (in Africa, at Disney's Animal Kingdom; $21 adults, $12 children; daily park opening–10:30am).

- At the **Garden Grill** ★ (in the Land Pavilion at Epcot; dinner $33 adults, $15 children; daily 4pm–park closing), hearty, family-style meals are hosted by Mickey and Chip 'n' Dale. (Mickey sure gets around, eh?)

- **1900 Park Fare** ★ (4401 Floridian Way, at Disney's Grand Floridian Resort & Spa; breakfast $22 adults, $13 children; dinner $36 adults, $18 children; daily 8–11:10am and 4:30–8:20pm) offers breakfast (eggs, French toast, bacon, pancakes) and dinner buffets (steak, pork, fish). Mary Poppins, Alice in Wonderland, and friends appear at breakfast; Cinderella and friends show up for Cinderella's Gala Feast at dinner.

- At **'Ohana** (p. 93; $25 adults, $14 children; daily 7:30–11am), traditional breakfasts (eggs, pancakes, bacon) are prepared in a fire pit and served family style. Mickey, Stitch, Lilo, and Pluto appear, and children are given the chance to parade around with Polynesian musical instruments.

# Exploring Walt Disney World

The minute someone even mentions Walt Disney World, most people's minds immediately conjure up visions of Cinderella Castle and the Magic Kingdom. That's not surprising when you take into account that the park that started it all—it opened in 1971—is still the most widely recognized and the most popular Disney destination in the United States.

Today, however, Walt Disney World has grown to include an array of themed resorts, hundreds of restaurants and shops, night-club venues, smaller attractions, and four major theme parks: the Magic Kingdom, Epcot, Disney's Hollywood Studios, and Animal Kingdom.

And even with an uncertain economy, park attendance continues to rise. WDW attracted more than 51 million paying customers in 2009, according to estimates by TEA, Inc., and Economic Research Associates. All four Disney parks make the country's top five in attendance list (the remaining park on the list is Disneyland in CA). The Disney Imagineers show off their creative capabilities through spectacular parades and fireworks displays, 3-D and CircleVision films, nerve-racking thrill rides, and adventurous journeys through time and space. Though still expensive, you'll seldom hear people complain about failing to get their money's worth—at home, an evening out, including dinner, a movie, and a babysitter, can add up to a hefty amount without the same return (though that price comparison is not as positive as it used to be).

To keep you coming back for more, rides and shows are periodically updated, new experiences are added, and unique (often spectacular) yearlong parkwide celebrations periodically add to the mix.

# 1 ESSENTIALS

## GETTING TO WDW BY CAR

The interstate exits to all Disney parks and resorts are well marked. Once you're off I-4, signs direct you to individual destinations. Drive with extra caution in the attractions area.

Upon entering WDW grounds, you can tune your radio to 1030 AM when you're approaching the Magic Kingdom, or 850 AM when approaching Epcot, for park information. Tune to 1200 AM when departing the Magic Kingdom, or 910 AM when departing Epcot. TVs in all Disney resorts and "official" hotels also have park information channels.

### Parking

All WDW lots are tightly controlled; the Disney folks have parking down to a science. You park where they tell you to park—and there's no room for discussion. *Remember to write your parking place (lot and row number) on something so you can find your vehicle later.*

Visitors should generally ride the free trams that travel the massive Magic Kingdom lots, but it's often easier to skip them and walk to the gates at Epcot, Disney's Hollywood Studios, and Animal Kingdom. You may not even have a choice. Disney has cut service to some parking areas near the entrances to its parks. Guests who can't make the hike have to park in special lots for travelers with disabilities (see below) or have a driver drop them at special unloading areas outside the entrances. If you're walking, *be careful!* These lots aren't designed for pedestrians, so if you hear a tram coming, move out of the way—and quickly.

Parking costs $14 at the four major WDW attractions ($15 for RVs). Parking is free to those staying at Disney-owned resorts. There are special lots for travelers with disabilities; a valid disabled parking permit is required (call ☎ 407/824-4321 for details). Those who have booked their Disney vacation through AAA can access a special lot close to the entrance.

Disney's ticketing structure (called **Magic Your Way**), gives visitors who stay here for a few days far better deals than those who come for just a day. The system allows guests to customize their tickets by first purchasing a Base Ticket for a set fee, and then allowing them to purchase add-ons, including a ParkHopper option, a no-expiration option, and the option to include admission to some of Disney's smaller venues, such as the water parks.

You can purchase your Base Tickets for durations running from a single day to several days, with the latter being the most cost effective; the longer you stay, the less you'll pay per day. If you crunch the numbers, tickets good for at least 4 days will cost at least $24 less per day than a single-day ticket would; buy a 6-day ticket and your per-day price drops by just under 50%. Do note, however, that under the new system, tickets now expire 14 days from the first day of use unless you add on a no-expiration feature (however, you don't have to use the tickets on consecutive days within that 14-day period).

The following prices **don't** include the *6.5% to 7% sales tax* (Disney actually falls in two different counties) unless noted. *Note:* Price hikes are frequent occurrences, so call (© **407/824-4321**) or visit WDW's website (www.disneyworld.com) for the most up-to-the-minute pricing.

*Note:* All tickets include unlimited use of the WDW transportation system. Bear in mind that Disney considers children 10 and older to be adults for pricing purposes, and children younger than 3 aren't charged admission.

**One-day/one-park Base Tickets,** for admission to the Magic Kingdom, Epcot, Animal Kingdom, or Disney's Hollywood Studios, are $82 for adults, $74 for children ages 3 to 9. Ouch! **Four-day Base Tickets** (one park per day) are $232 adults, $209 children ages 3 to 9. **Seven-day Base Tickets** (one park per day) cost$247 for adults (just over $35 a day), $224 for kids ages 3 to 9 (about $32 a day).

Adding on a **Park Hopper** option to your ticket allows you unlimited admission to the Magic Kingdom, Epcot, Animal Kingdom, and

# Walt Disney World Parks & Attractions

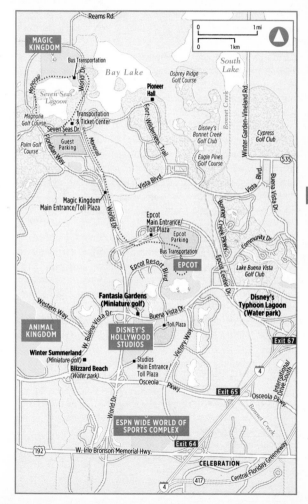

Disney's Hollywood Studios for the duration of your Base Ticket. Pricing for the Park Hopper is the same for adults and children and costs $54 above the price of your Base Ticket (no matter how many days that ticket is valid for). So if you purchase a single-day Base Ticket, adding the Park Hopper will cost an additional $54 (for a total of $136 for an adult—not cost effective), but if you purchase a 7-day Base Ticket, the option will still only cost you $54 (for a total of $301—a good deal).

If you add a **Water Park Fun & More** option to your Base Ticket, you'll get several admissions to some of WDW's smaller attractions: Blizzard Beach, Typhoon Lagoon, DisneyQuest, Disney's Oak Trail Golf Course, and the ESPN Wide World of Sports Complex (Disney's Wide World of Sports in a past life). The number of visits allowed depends on the number of days your Base Ticket is good for (two visits for Base Tickets good for either 1 or 2 days; three visits for a 3-day base ticket, four visits for a 4-day base ticket, and so on; the number of visits equaling the number of days your base ticket is good for). This option adds an additional $54 to the cost of your Base Ticket, and, like the Park Hopper, the longer you stay at Disney, the more cost-effective the option becomes. If you plan on visiting only one smaller attraction (visiting only once) while at WDW, paying the separate admission fee is cheaper and smarter than opting for the Water Park Fun & More add-on.

A 1-day ticket to **Typhoon Lagoon** or **Blizzard Beach** is $46 for adults, $40 for children. A 1-day ticket to DisneyQuest is $42 for adults, $36 for children.

If you're planning an extended stay or going to visit Walt Disney World more than once during the year, **annual passes** ($499–$629 adults, $450–$567 children) are another great option (FL residents catch a slight break; $379–$499 adults, $342–$450 children).

## OPERATING HOURS

Hours of operation vary throughout the year and are often influenced by special events, so it's a good idea to call to check opening/closing times.

The **Magic Kingdom** and **Disney's Hollywood Studios** are generally open from 9am to 7 or 8pm, with hours often extended to 9pm and sometimes as late as midnight—even 1am during major holidays and summer. **Animal Kingdom** usually is open from 9am to 5 or 6pm but sometimes closes as late as 8pm.

**Epcot's Future World** is generally open from 9am to 7pm and occasionally later. **Epcot's World Showcase** usually opens at 11am and closes at 9pm. Once again, there are extended holiday and summer hours.

**Typhoon Lagoon** and **Blizzard Beach** are open from 10am to 5pm most of the year (with slightly extended hours during summer and some holidays). Both are closed on a rotating basis during part of the winter for maintenance; be sure to check ahead if they're on your to-do list.

# 2 MAKING YOUR VISIT MORE ENJOYABLE

## HOW THIS CHAPTER IS USEFUL TO PARENTS

Before every listing in the major parks, you'll note the **"Recommended Ages"** entry that lists which ages will most appreciate that ride or show (though you should keep in mind your child's personality and maturity when evaluating these recommendations). Though most families want to do everything, these guidelines are helpful in planning your daily itinerary. In my ride ratings, I indicate

---

 **Tips** **Price Alert**

Annual price increases are normal, so, although the prices listed on these pages were accurate when this book went to press, they may be higher at the time you actually visit.

## (Tips) FASTPASS

"Get a time—why wait in line . . . ," says Disney. If lines aren't your thing—well . . . you had better turn back now. Lines are a part of the deal at Disney. On the other hand, if you're savvy, you can usually avoid the worst of them if you take advantage of Disney's FASTPASS system. The free system allows you to wait on a far shorter line at some of the park's most popular attractions. Seems easy enough, right? Well, it is. There is, however, a small price to be paid for skipping the big lines. Here's the drill:

*Hang onto your ticket stub* when you enter and head to the hottest ride on your list. If it's a FASTPASS attraction (they're noted in the guide map you get when you enter), you'll see a sign marking the FASTPASS kiosk just near the entrance. Feed your ticket into the ticket taker. *Note:* Every member of your group must get an individual FASTPASS. Retrieve both your ticket and your FASTPASS slip. Printed on the slip are two times. You can return anytime during that 1-hour window and enter the ride (there's a much shorter and faster line for FASTPASS holders). Be sure to keep your slip handy as you'll need it to get in the right line.

whether a ride will be more enjoyable for kids than for adults. Many, even a couple in the Magic Kingdom, are too intense for young kids; all it takes is one bad experience, and the rest of your day will be ruined. You'll also find any **height and health restrictions** noted in the listings.

## PLAN YOUR VISIT

How you plan your time at Walt Disney World will depend on a number of factors. These include the ages of any children in your

***Note II:*** Early in the day, your 1-hour window may begin as soon as 40 minutes after you feed the FASTPASS machine, but later in the day it may be hours later. Initially, Disney only allowed you to do this on one ride at a time. Now, your FAST-PASS ticket has a time printed when you can get a second FASTPASS, usually about 2 hours after you got the first one, though it can sometimes be as soon as 45 minutes later, even if you haven't used the first pass yet.

***Note III:*** Don't think you can fool Disney by feeding your ticket stub in multiple times, figuring you can hit the jackpot for multiple rides or help others in your group who lost their tickets. These "smart" stubs will reject your attempts by spitting out a coupon that says "Not a Valid FASTPASS."

***Note IV:*** FASTPASS slips can run out. So if you have your heart set on a ride and it's the middle of the peak season, be sure to head to your chosen attraction's FASTPASS machine as soon as you can. Tickets for top rides often run out by the early afternoon, sometimes even earlier.

party; what, if anything, you've seen on previous visits; your interests; and whether you're traveling at peak time or off season. Preplanning is always essential. So is choosing age-appropriate activities.

Nothing can spoil a day in the parks more than a child devastated because he or she can't do something that was promised. Before you get to the park, review this book and the suggested ages for children, including *height restrictions.* The WDW staff won't bend the rules despite the pitiful wails of your little ones. ***Note:*** Many rides that have minimum heights also have enough turbulence to make them unsuitable for folks with neck, back, or heart problems; those prone to motion sickness; or pregnant women.

Unless you're staying for more than a week or two, you won't be able to experience all of the rides, shows, or attractions included in this chapter. A ride may last only 5 minutes, but you may have to wait an hour or so, even with FASTPASS (detailed shortly). You'll wear yourself to a frazzle trying to hit everything. It's better to follow a relaxed itinerary, including leisurely meals and some recreational activities, than to make a demanding job out of trying to see everything. Your vacation is supposed to be fun, not frenzied.

## CREATE AN ITINERARY FOR EACH DAY

Read the previously mentioned *Walt Disney World Vacations* brochure and the detailed descriptions in this book, and then create your own "must-see" list, including all the shows and attractions that you absolutely have to experience. After that, you can sort out just where to go, when to go, and what you would like to do while you're there.

At the same time, consider your loyalties. Put the ride featuring your favorite character, or theirs, at the top of your list. Sketch out a daily itinerary that includes your must-see attractions and shows; it's almost certain to change once you get to the parks, but will at least provide you with a good starting point. With a plan in mind and a map in hand (be sure to grab the free maps distributed as you enter each theme park), touring the parks will be that much easier. Understand that rides and exhibits nearest an entrance are usually the busiest when the gates open because a lot of people visit the first thing they see, even if the more popular attractions tend to be found deeper into the park.

I repeat this advice: Schedule sit-down shows, recreational activities (a boat ride or a refreshing swim late in the afternoon), and at least some unhurried meals where time permits. This will save you from exhaustion and aggravation. If you have the luxury of a multiday pass, you can divide and conquer at a slower pace and can even repeat some favorites.

# 3 THE MAGIC KINGDOM

The Magic Kingdom still attracts millions from around the world, drawn here by the opportunity to experience the fun and fantasy that only Disney can deliver. The 107-acre Magic Kingdom is filled with more than 40 attractions (with new experiences being added almost yearly), unique shops, and themed restaurants. Its most recognizable feature is Cinderella Castle, the park's icon and centerpiece. And surrounding the castle are the park's **seven themed lands,** stretching out like the spokes of a wheel.

**ARRIVING** The parking lot here is huge—so big, in fact, that it's necessary to take a tram just to get to the **Transportation and Ticket Center** (more commonly known as the TTC), where you can buy your park tickets. Each of the parking lot's sections is named for Disney characters (Goofy, Pluto, Minnie, and so on), and aisles are numbered. I can't stress enough just how important it is *to write down where you left your vehicle—you would be amazed at how many white minivans look just like yours!* Once you have your tickets in hand (or if you've arrived with them—the best route), you'll need to make your first decision of the day—do you take the ferry or the monorail to the park from the TTC? The ferry offers a more leisurely (and windy) ride, while the monorail is the speedier of the two.

Upon arriving at the park entrance you will have to pass through security and have your bags inspected. All told, the time it takes to get from your car to Main Street U.S.A. is somewhere around **35 to 45 minutes,** sometimes longer. And that total doesn't include the time spent in lines if you have to stop at Guest Relations or rent a stroller. You'll face the same agony (complicated by escaping crowds) on the way out, so relax. This is one of the most crowded parks, so plan to arrive an hour before the opening bell or an hour or two after.

The most important thing you can do upon arriving at the park is to pick up a copy (or two) of the Magic Kingdom **guide map** (if you can't find one at the turnstiles, stop at the City Hall information center or the nearest shop). It provides an array of detailed information about available guest services, restaurants, and attractions. The *Times Guide* (separate from the guide map) will be your key to the daily schedules for showtimes, parades, fireworks, character meet-and-greets, and park and restaurant hours.

## SERVICES & FACILITIES IN THE MAGIC KINGDOM

Most of the following are noted on the handout guide maps in the park:

**ATMS** Machines inside the park are near the main entrance; in Frontierland, near the Shootin' Gallery; and in Tomorrowland, next to Space Mountain.

**BABY CARE** Located next to the Crystal Palace at the end of Main Street, the Baby Care Center is furnished with a nursing room with rocking chairs and toddler-size toilets.

**FIRST AID** It's located beside the Crystal Palace next to the Baby Care Center and staffed by registered nurses.

**LOST CHILDREN** Lost children in the Magic Kingdom are usually taken to City Hall or the Baby Care Center. *Children younger than 7 should wear name-tags inside their clothing.*

**PETS** It's illegal to leave yours in a parked car, even with a window cracked open; cars become ovenlike death traps in Florida's sun. Only service animals are permitted in the parks, but there are five (soon to be six) kennels at WDW (© **407/824-6568;** $13–$23 per day, depending on whether your pet is staying overnight and whether you are a Disney resort guest). All centers offer both day accommodations and overnight boarding. *Proof of vaccination is required.* For more information, see chapter 7, "Fast Facts."

**STROLLERS** They can be rented at the Stroller Shop near the entrance to the Magic Kingdom. The cost is $15 for a single and $31 for a double with length-of-stay rentals available for $13 per day for a single and $27 per day for a double. Full payment is required up front for a length-of-stay rental.

approximate waiting time at all of the major rides and attractions. In Magic Kingdom it's at the end of Main Street on the left as you face the castle.

**WHEELCHAIR RENTAL**    For wheelchairs, go to the gift shop to the left of the ticket booths at the Transportation and Ticket Center, or to the Stroller and Wheelchair Shop inside the main entrance to your right. The cost is $12 for a regular wheelchair; $50, plus a $20 refundable deposit, for electric convenience vehicles.

## MAIN STREET, U.S.A.

Designed to model a turn-of-the-20th-century American street (though it ends in a 13th-c. European castle), this is the gateway to the Kingdom. Don't dawdle on Main Street (it's filled mostly with shops and restaurants) when you enter; leave it for the end of the day when you're heading back to your hotel.

### Main Street Vehicles

**Frommer's Rating:** C

**Recommended Ages:** Mainly nostalgic adults or toddlers

Ride a horse-drawn trolley, jitney, vintage fire engine, or horseless carriage *only* if you don't mind waiting around for a bit. While a nice little diversion, there are far more interesting things to see and do throughout the realm.

### Walt Disney World Railroad

**Frommer's Rating:** B

**Recommended Ages:** All ages

Climb aboard an authentic 1928 steam-powered train for a relaxing, 15-minute tour of the perimeter of the park. This is a great way to entertain the younger kids in your family while the older ones are off taking in some of Disney's more thrilling attractions. It's also a good way for kids and adults alike to rest for a brief moment while taking in the surrounding sights. There are a total of three stations: at the park entrance, at Frontierland, and at Mickey's Toontown Fair.

## Frommer's Rates the Rides

Because there's so much to do, we're shifting from the star-rating system used for rooms and restaurants to one that has a bit more range. You'll notice most of the grades below are *As, Bs,* and *Cs.* That's because Disney designers have done a reasonably good job on the attractions front. But occasionally our ratings show *Ds* for Duds.

Here's what **Frommer's Ratings** mean:

**A+** = Your trip wouldn't be complete without it.
**A** = Put it at the top of your "to-do" list.
**B+** = Make a real effort to see or do it.
**B** = It's fun but not a "must see."
**C+** = A nice diversion; see it if you have time.
**C** = Go if there's no wait and you can walk right in.
**D** = Don't bother.

And while you're cruising down Main Street, be on the lookout for the **Dapper Dans,** a lively barbershop quartet that harmonizes its way up and down the boulevard.

### Shopping on Main Street

Shopping at Disney has almost become a pastime in and of itself, and the largest collection of shops in the Kingdom is located right along Main Street, U.S.A. The **Emporium,** in Town Square, has the park's largest selection of Disneyana. Stop by and pick up some of the more unique sweets and treats at the **Main Street Confectionary** or some shiny baubles at **Uptown Jewelers.**

## ADVENTURELAND

Cross a bridge marked by tikis and torches as the rhythm of beating drums sounds in the distance. As you make your way through lush jungle foliage, trees hung with Spanish moss, dense vines, and

stands of palm and bamboo, you are transported to an exotic locale
where swashbuckling adventures await.

### The Enchanted Tiki Room—Under New Management

**Frommer's Rating:** B for kids, C for adults in need of an amusing break

**Recommended Ages:** 2–10 and older adults

The Tiki Room serves up a Polynesian atmosphere, with its thatched roof, bamboo beams, tapa-bark murals, and torches. Inside guests are entertained by the likes of Iago (from *Aladdin*) and Zazu (from *The Lion King*), as well as an ensemble of boisterous tropical birds (more than 200 of them, in fact), along with chanting totem poles and singing flowers that whistle, warble, and tweet. Overall, it's good family fun, but be aware that it's rather loud, and the multitude of audio and visual effects may be a bit too overwhelming for very young children.

### Jungle Cruise

**Frommer's Rating:** C+ (B for the foot-weary)

**Recommended Ages:** 4–adult

This 10-minute ride's slower pace is a yawner for many older kids and teens, but it's a nice break from the madness if the line isn't long or you use FASTPASS. You'll sail through the African veldt in the Congo, an Amazon rainforest, and along the Nile in Egypt as your boat captain offers somewhat corny but humorous commentary on your travels. You'll encounter dozens of exotic animatronic animals, ranging from playful elephants to lions and tigers, as you sail through dense tropical and subtropical foliage (most of it is real). You'll pass a Cambodian temple guarded by snakes, a rhino chasing terrified African beaters as they clamor up a totem pole for safety, and a jungle camp taken over by apes.

### Magic Carpets of Aladdin

**Frommer's Rating:** A for tykes and parents

**Recommended Ages:** 2–8

Younger kids will appreciate this ride's gentle ups and downs as they fly through the sky on the colorful magic carpets. The view of Agrabah from above is impressive, but be prepared as you make your way around the genie's giant bottle—the spitting camels have pretty good aim, making it likely that you'll get squirted with water. There are only 16 four-passenger fiberglass carpets on the ride, which can make for extremely long lines (though not nearly as unbearable as some you'll encounter in Fantasyland).

## Pirates of the Caribbean

**Frommer's Rating:** A

**Recommended Ages:** 6–adult

The release of *Pirates of the Caribbean: The Curse of the Black Pearl* and its recent sequels, *Dead Man's Chest* and *At World's End,* has revitalized the popularity of this oldie but goodie. They also inspired the recent renovations that now have Jack Sparrow and Barbossa joining the original set of swashbucklers. A tweak in the storyline to better mirror the movie, and a mix of new and updated special effects have been added, too. Still, the ride might be a bit scary for kids younger than 5 due to an unexpected yet small waterfall and moments of darkness.

After making your way through dark and dank dungeons, guests board a boat and set sail for a small Caribbean town, its shores teeming with pillaging animatronic pirates. There's plenty of gunfire and cannonballs fly through the air as the marauders battle each other, with you, of course, caught in the middle. The effects are great, as is the yo-ho-ho music of "A Pirate's Life for Me" that plays in the background.

The bonus here is an immense covered queue area that will protect you and your stroller-bound children from both sun and rain (this ride offers the only covered stroller parking in the park). *Tip:* Nod hello to the parrot (Peg-legged Pete) above the entrance plaza and he may offer you his own greeting.

## Swiss Family Treehouse

**Frommer's Rating:** C

**Recommended Ages:** 4–12

This attraction, based on the 1960 Disney movie version of *Swiss Family Robinson,* includes a few more comforts from home than did the original. After climbing its many, many steps, you'll finally reach the treehouse, its rooms filled with mahogany furnishings, decorative accents, and running water. If you're nervous about heights, this one's not for you—visitors will find themselves walking along a rope-suspended bridge high above the ground, not to mention the climbing that's required to make it up and down all the stairs that lead around this 50-foot banyan tree. The "tree," designed by Disney Imagineers, has 330,000 polyethylene leaves sprouting from a 90-foot span of branches; although it isn't real, it's draped with actual Spanish moss. *Note:* People with limited mobility beware—this attraction requires a lot of climbing.

## Shopping in Adventureland
Located at the Pirates of the Caribbean exit, the **Pirates Bazaar** is filled with everything a child needs to play pirate, from hats to hooks and everything in between.

## FRONTIERLAND
From Adventureland you'll step into the wild and woolly past of the American frontier, where the sidewalks are wooden; rough-and-tumble architecture runs to log cabins and rustic saloons; and the landscape is Southwestern scrubby with mesquite, cactus, yucca, and prickly pear.

### Big Thunder Mountain Railroad
**Frommer's Rating:** A
**Recommended Ages:** 8–adult
This roller coaster earns high marks for what it is—a ride designed for those not quite up to the lunch-losing thrills of the **Rock 'n' Roller Coaster** at Disney's Hollywood Studios (p. 158). Think of Big Thunder as *Roller Coasters 101.* (Survive and graduate to the next level.) It sports fun hairpin turns and dark descents rather than sudden, steep drops and near collisions. Your runaway train covers 2,780 feet of track and careens through the ribs of a dinosaur, under a thundering waterfall, past spewing geysers, and over a bottomless volcanic pool. Animatronic characters (such as a long john–clad fellow in a bathtub) and critters (goats, chickens, donkeys) enhance the scenic backdrop, along with several hundred thousand dollars' worth of authentic antique mining equipment. *Note:* You must be at least 40 inches tall to ride, and Disney

## (Tips) Riding the Rails

Although it's an oldie, Big Thunder Mountain Railroad is still a magnet for the masses. If a FASTPASS isn't available (and that can happen), try riding it late in the day (coaster veterans swear the ride is even better after dark) or during one of the parades that draw visitors away from the attractions.

discourages expectant mothers, people prone to motion sickness, or those with heart, neck, or back problems from riding.

### Country Bear Jamboree
**Frommer's Rating:** B+
**Recommended Ages:** 3–adult; though the younger the child, the better

This is a foot-stomping hoot! It opened as one of the park's original attractions way back when in 1971, a time when entertainment was more low-tech but fun just the same. The 15-minute show stars a backwoods troupe of fiddlin', strummin', harmonica-playin' bears (all audio-animatronic, of course) belting out lively tunes and woeful love songs. The chubby Trixie, decked out in a satiny skirt, laments lost love as she sings "Tears Will Be the Chaser for Your Wine." Teddi Barra descends from the ceiling in a swing to perform "Heart, We Did All That We Could." Big Al moans "Blood in the Saddle." In the finale, the cast joins in a rousing sing-along. *Blue-light bonus:* The jamboree is a great summertime place to cool your heels in the A/C.

### Frontierland Shootin' Arcade
**Frommer's Rating:** C
**Recommended Ages:** 8–adult

Combining state-of-the-art electronics with a traditional shooting-gallery format, this arcade presents an array of targets (slow-moving ore cars, buzzards, and gravediggers) in an 1850s boomtown scenario. Fog creeps across the graveyard, and the setting changes as a calm, starlit night turns stormy with flashes of lightning and claps of thunder. Coyotes howl, bridges creak, and skeletal arms reach out from the grave. If you hit a tombstone, it might spin around and mysteriously change its epitaph. To keep things authentic, newfangled electronic firing mechanisms loaded with infrared bullets are concealed in vintage buffalo rifles. A dollar buys you 35 shots. Though it's a pretty cool arcade, there are far better ways to spend your time in Magic Kingdom.

### Splash Mountain

**Frommer's Rating:** A+

**Recommended Ages:** 8–adult

If you need a quick cooling off, this is the place to go—because you will get wet (though it's hit or miss whether you get damp or drenched)! Based on Disney's 1946 film *Song of the South,* Splash Mountain takes you flume-style down a flooded mountain, past 26 colorful scenes that include backwoods swamps, bayous, spooky caves, and waterfalls. Riders are caught in the bumbling schemes of Brer Fox and Brer Bear as they chase the ever-wily Brer Rabbit. The music from the film forms a delightful audio backdrop. Your hollow-log vehicle twists, turns, and splashes, sometimes plummeting in darkness as the ride leads to a 52-foot, 45-degree, 40-mph splashdown in a briar-filled pond (you'll feel the drop!). *Note:* You must be at least 40 inches tall to ride. Also, expectant mothers and people prone to motion sickness or those with heart, neck, or back problems shouldn't climb aboard.

### Tom Sawyer Island

**Frommer's Rating:** C for most, B+ for energetic kids who need a release

**Recommended Ages:** 4–12

Huck Finn's raft will take you on a 2-minute journey across the River of America to the densely forested Tom Sawyer Island, where kids can explore the narrow passages of Injun Joe's cave, walk through a windmill, examine a serpentine abandoned mine, and investigate Fort Longhorn. The island's two bridges—one a suspension bridge, the other made of barrels floating on top of the water—create quite a challenge for anyone trying to cross. Maintaining your balance is

## ⓣ Tips  A (Baker's) Dozen Suggestions for Fewer Headaches

1. **Be a Leader, Not a Follower:** Try going against the grain and head left toward Adventureland to begin your day (most visitors sprint for Tomorrowland). If you have the time and aren't a slave to the compressed itinerary of a 1-day visit, make your way to one (maybe two) major attractions early on; then save the others for early on your second day when crowds are lightest.

2. **Note Your Car's Location:** That bright yellow Hummer in the next space may not be there when you get out. Write your lot and row number on something with ink that won't run if it gets wet.

3. **Avoid the Rush:** I-4 can get horribly crowded at times, so be ready for bumper-to-bumper traffic from 7 to 9am, 4 to 7pm, and often in between. Check your map for alternate routes, and try to leave the parks a half-hour before closing.

4. **Be Realistic:** As a group, list three or four "must-do" things each day. If you can, consider splitting up, with each adult taking one or more kids—one heading for the thrill rides, the other for the tamer, tot-friendly attractions.

5. **Timing Is Everything:** Relax—the park isn't going anywhere. And rushing just to wait in line seems rather silly, doesn't it? Once inside the park, mix it up a bit; stagger the attraction lines with indoor shows or even breaks on a shady bench.

6. **Call Ahead:** If a sit-down dinner in a special restaurant is important to you, be sure to make Advance Reservations (ⓒ **407/939-3463**) before your visit.

7. **Set a Spending Limit:** Kids should know they have a set amount to spend on take-home trinkets. You should, too. Sticking to your budget will be beneficial in the

end, but building in a small contingency "fun" fund for emergencies is still a good idea.

8. **Take a Break:** If you're staying at a WDW property, spend midafternoon napping (don't laugh, you may need one) or unwinding in your resort's pool. Return to the parks for a few more attractions and the closing shows. (Get your hand stamped when you leave, and you'll be readmitted without charge.)

9. **Dress Comfortably:** This may seem like common sense, but judging by the limping, blistered crowds trudging the parks, most people don't understand the immeasurable amount of walking they'll be doing. Wear comfortable, broken-in walking shoes or sneakers.

10. **Don't Skimp on the Sunscreen:** The Florida sun can be relentless, even in the shade, under the clouds, or in the cooler months. Dress appropriately—wear lightweight, light-colored clothing, and bring along hats (especially for toddlers and infants, even if they'll be in a stroller). If you must show off your skin, slather it in sunscreen (with at least a 30 SPF).

11. **Travel Light:** Don't carry large amounts of cash. The Pirates of the Caribbean aren't the only thieves in WDW. There are ATMs in the parks and most resorts if you run short.

12. **Get a Little Goofy:** Relax, put on those mouse ears, eat that extra piece of fudge, and sing along at the shows. Don't worry about what the staff thinks; they've seen it all (and they're dressed pretty goofily, too).

13. **Take Measure of Your Kids:** This guide, park maps, and information boards outside the more adventurous rides list minimum heights. Trust me—WDW won't budge because of sad faces or temper tantrums when your safety is involved.

**Tips** **Parental Touring Tip**

Many of the attractions at Walt Disney World offer a **Parent Switch program,** designed for parents traveling with small children. While one parent rides an attraction, the other stays with kids not quite ready to handle the experience; then the adults switch places without having to stand in line again. The bonus (beyond the obvious) is that the kids able to ride the attraction will get to ride again, too. Notify a cast member if you wish to participate when you get in line.

difficult at best, if (or should I say when) the other guests are jumping up and down—but that's half the fun. Narrow, winding dirt paths lined with oaks, pines, and sycamores create an authentic backwoods atmosphere. It's easy to get briefly lost and stumble upon some unexpected adventure, but for younger children, the woods and caves can pose a real problem—toddlers who can't easily find their way back to you or who may get scared by darkness and eerie noises should be watched very carefully. Aunt Polly's Dockside Inn, though open only seasonally, serves up sweet treats and snacks, and with a porch overlooking the river makes the perfect spot to sit and relax after all that running around.

### Shopping in Frontierland

Mosey into the **Frontier Trading Post** for the latest and greatest in cowboy wear. The **Prairie Outpost and Supply** is your best bet for sweets and treats.

## LIBERTY SQUARE

Unlike the other lands in Magic Kingdom, Liberty Square doesn't have clearly delineated boundaries. Pass through Frontierland into this small area, and you'll suddenly find yourself in the middle of Colonial America. Before you can say "George Washington," you'll be standing in front of the Liberty Tree, an immense live oak decorated with 13 lanterns symbolizing the first 13 colonies. The entire area has an 18th-century, early American feel, complete with Federal and Georgian architecture, quaint shops, and flowerbeds bordering manicured lawns. The **Liberty Tree Tavern** (p. 78) is one of the better Magic Kingdom restaurants.

## Hall of Presidents

**Frommer's Rating:** B+

**Recommended Ages:** 8–adult

American presidents from George Washington to Barack Obama are represented by lifelike audio-animatronic figures (arguably the best in WDW). If you look closely, you'll see them fidget and whisper during the performance. The show begins with a film projected on a 180-degree, 70mm screen. It talks about the importance of the Constitution, then the curtain rises on America's leaders, and, as each comes into the spotlight, he nods or waves with presidential dignity. Lincoln then rises and speaks, occasionally referring to his notes.

## Haunted Mansion

**Frommer's Rating:** A

**Recommended Ages:** 6–adult

What better way to show off Disney's eye for detailed special effects than through this oldie but goodie (Walt had a hand in its development), where "Grim Grinning Ghosts" come out to socialize—or so the ride's theme song goes. Upon entering, you're greeted by a ghostly host, who encloses you in a windowless portrait gallery where the floor seems to descend (actually, it's the ceiling that's rising) and the room goes dark (the only truly scary moment). Darkness, spooky music, eerie howling, and mysterious screams and rappings enhance its ambience. Your vehicle, err, Doom Buggy takes you past a ghostly banquet and ball, a graveyard band, a suit of armor that comes alive, a ghostly talking head in a crystal ball, and more. Thanks to a rather lengthy rehab in 2007, the ghosts are even ghoulier, the spectral special effects more spectacular, and the sinister silliness . . . well, you get the picture. Overall, the experience is more amusing than terrifying; most children 6 and older

> **Fun Facts**   **It's a Dirty Job . . .**
>
> The Disney parks are usually fairly clean, but there's one notable spot in the Magic Kingdom that takes pride in its dreary image. In order to maintain the Haunted Mansion's weathered and worn appearance, employees spread large amounts of dust over the home's interior and also string up plenty of real-looking cobwebs. It takes a lot of effort to keep the place looking bedraggled, which may explain why your haunted hosts are only a handful of Disney cast members without smiles plastered on their faces.

will be fine, but those younger (and even some of the older ones) may not be so amused.

**Liberty Square Riverboat** (Overrated

**Frommer's Rating:** C

**Recommended Ages:** All ages

The *Liberty Belle*, a grand steam-powered riverboat (recently refurbished in order to retain its stature as such), offers lazy 17-minute cruises along the Rivers of America, allowing thrill-ride-weary passengers the chance to rest and relax. As you pass along the shores of Frontierland, the Indian camp, wildlife, and wilderness cabin will make it seem as if you're traveling through the wild and wooly West.

## Shopping in Liberty Square

The **Heritage House** is filled with replicas of famous documents (they're great for school projects), including the Declaration of Independence; miniature models of the Statue of Liberty; and everything Americana, from souvenir spoons and campaign buttons to flags and red-white-and-blue T-shirts. **Ye Olde Christmas Shoppe,** filled with decorations and Disney ornaments galore, celebrates Christmas every day of the year.

The most fanciful land in the park, Fantasyland features attractions that bring classic Disney characters to life. It is by far the most popular land in the park for young children, who can sail over Merry Ole' London and Never Never Land, ride in a honey pot through the Hundred-Acre Wood, and fly with Dumbo. If your kids are younger than 8, you'll find yourself spending a lot of your time here (and at Mickey's Toontown Fair, detailed later in this section). *Note:* At press time, Disney had broken ground on what is being touted as the largest expansion in the history of the Magic Kingdom—the expansion of Fantasyland. Over the next 3 years (with a completion date set for 2013), new rides, attractions, character experiences, and restaurants will be added; each princess will get her own themed village within the newly created Fantasyland Forest.

## Cinderella Castle (Moments)

**Frommer's Rating:** A (for visuals)

**Recommended Ages:** All ages

There's actually not a lot to do here, but it's the Magic Kingdom's most widely recognized symbol, and I guarantee that you won't be able to pass it by without a look. It's not as if you could miss it anyway. The fairy-tale castle looms over Main Street, U.S.A., its 189-foot-high Gothic spires taking center stage from the minute you enter the park.

One of the most popular restaurants in the park is set inside the castle, **Cinderella's Royal Table** (p. 76), along with the **Bibiddi Bobiddi Boutique** (p. 124). Elaborate mosaic murals depict the Cinderella story in the castle's archway, and Disney family coats of arms are displayed over a fireplace. An actress portraying Cinderella, dressed for the ball, often makes appearances in the lobby. The Castle Forecourt Stage features live shows daily so be sure to check the daily *Times Guide*'s schedule for **Dream Along with Mickey.** Disney's latest outdoor stage show is an entertainer that features singing and dancing by Mickey, Peter Pan, Captain Hook, and plenty of other familiar favorites (both good and evil).

## (Tips) A Swish of the Wand

If you've been to Disney lately, it's difficult not to notice the ever increasing number of pint-sized princesses wandering about the world. These magical makeovers (for kids ages 3 and up) are all the rage thanks to Disney's new **Bibiddi Bobiddi Boutique** (the original boutique located in Downtown Disney, the newest located in Cinderella Castle at the Magic Kingdom). The boutique, run by Fairy-Godmothers in training, is open daily from 9am to 5pm, and reservations are practically a must ((C) **407/ 939-7895**).

Princess package options include the **Coach** (hair styling, shimmering makeup, and a princess sash for $49.95 plus tax), the **Crown** (hair styling, shimmering makeup, nails, and a princess sash for $59.95 plus tax), and the **Castle Package** (hair styling, shimmering makeup, nails, a princess sash, and an entire princess costume complete with shoes, crown, magic wand, and photos for between $189.95-$249.95 plus tax). The **Cool Dude**, great for little brothers who have to wait it out with sis, includes hair styling, colored gels and sparkles, or a Mickey stencil for $7.50.

**Prince Charming Regal Carrousel** (Moments)
**Frommer's Rating:** B+ for younger kids, A for carousel fans
**Recommended Ages:** All ages

One of the most beautiful attractions at Disney—and known until 2010 as **Cinderella's Golden Carrousel**—this one is as enchanting to look at as it is to ride. Originally built by the Philadelphia Toboggan Co. in 1917, the carousel toured many an amusement park in the Midwest long before Walt Disney bought it and brought it to Orlando 5 years before the Magic Kingdom opened.

Disney artisans meticulously refurbished it, adding 18 hand-painted scenes from Cinderella on a wooden canopy above the horses. Its organ plays Disney classics such as "When You Wish Upon a Star." Adults and children alike adore riding the ornate horses round and round; there are even a few benches for the littlest tykes in the family. The ride is longer than you might expect, but the lines can get lengthy as well, so check back a bit later if your timing is off the first time around.

### Dumbo the Flying Elephant

**Frommer's Rating:** B+ for younger kids and parents

**Recommended Ages:** 2–6

This is a favorite of the preschool set, a fact that will quickly become apparent when you see the line wrapping around, and around, and around. Much like **Magic Carpets of Aladdin** (p. 113), the Dumbo vehicles fly around in a circle, gently rising and dipping as you control them from inside the elephant. If you can stand the brutal lines—extending well beyond the barely covered queue (there are gigantic fans, though I have yet to see them actually running) and out in the blazing sun—this ride is almost sure to make your little one's day. *Note:* Be aware that Dumbo is slated for a major overhaul during the Fantasyland expansion.

### it's a small world

**Frommer's Rating:** B+ for youngsters and first-timers

**Recommended Ages:** 2–8

Recently refurbished to spruce up some of its older displays, it's a small world is one of those rides that you just have to do because it's been there since the beginning—it's a classic (built for the 1964 World's Fair before being transplanted to Disney), and in this day and age it's nice to see that some things don't change (or at least not too much). If you don't know the song, you will by the end of the ride (and probably ever after), as the hard part is trying to get it *out* of your head. As you sail along you'll pass through the countries of the world, each filled with appropriately costumed audio-animatronic dolls greeting you by singing "It's a Small World" in tiny Munchkin voices. The cast of thousands includes Chinese acrobats, Russian kazachok dancers, Indian snake charmers, French cancan girls, and, well, you get the picture. To truly experience everything Disney, this one's a must.

### Mad Tea Party

**Frommer's Rating:** C+

**Recommended Ages:** 4–adult

Traditional amusement park ride it may be, but it's still a family favorite—maybe because it is so simple. The mad tea party scene in *Alice in Wonderland* was the inspiration for this one, and riders sit in giant pastel-colored teacups set on saucers that careen around a circular platform while the cup, saucer, and platform all spin round and round. Occasionally, the woozy Dormouse pops out of a big central teapot to see just what's going on. Tame as it may appear, this can be a pretty active, even nauseating ride, depending on how much you spin your teacup's wheel. Adolescents seem to consider it a badge of honor if they can turn the unsuspecting adults in their cup green—you have been warned!

### The Many Adventures of Winnie the Pooh

**Frommer's Rating:** B

**Recommended Ages:** 2–8 and their parents

When this replaced Mr. Toad's Wild Ride in 1999, it drew a small storm of protest from Toad lovers, but things have quieted since then. This fun ride features the cute and cuddly little fellow along with Eeyore, Piglet, and Tigger. You board a golden honey pot and ride through a storybook version of the Hundred-Acre Wood, keeping an eye out for Heffalumps, Woozles, Blustery Days, and the Floody Place. Young kids absolutely love it, but be prepared to brave some *very* long lines if you don't use FASTPASS. *Note:* Pooh's Playful Spot was closed at press time due to ongoing construction and the expansion of Fantasyland. If it's open when you visit, your tinier tots will enjoy the small play area filled with places to crawl, slide, and occasionally get wet.

### Mickey's PhilharMagic

**Frommer's Rating:** A+

**Recommended Ages:** All ages

This is by far the most amazing 3-D movie production I've ever laid eyes on and is a must-see for everyone. Popular Disney characters—

including Ariel, Simba, and Aladdin—are brought to 3-D life on a
150-foot screen (the largest wraparound screen on the planet) as they
try to help (or in some cases hinder) the attempts of Donald Duck
to retrieve Mickey's magical sorcerer's hat before the Mouse discovers
it's missing. It's the first time the classic Disney characters have ever
been rendered in 3-D. Even if you're not a big fan of shows, this is
one you should see. Like (but far better than) the whimsical **Jim
Henson's Muppet*Vision 3-D** (p. 164) at Disney's Hollywood
Studios, the show combines music, animated film, puppetry, and
special effects that tickle several of your senses. The kids will love the
animation and effects, and parents will enjoy the nostalgia factor.

### Peter Pan's Flight
**Frommer's Rating:** A for kids and parents
**Recommended Ages:** 3–8
Another of Disney's simple pleasures, this is a classic ride that's fun
for the whole family. You'll fly through the sky in your very own
ship (much like that of Captain Hook's), gliding over familiar
scenes from the adventures of Peter Pan. Your adventure begins in
the Darlings' nursery and includes a flight over an elaborate nighttime cityscape of Merry Ole' London, before you move on to
Never Land. There you encounter mermaids, Indians, Tick Tock
the Croc, the Lost Boys, Princess Tiger Lilly, Tinker Bell, Hook,
and Smee, all while listening to the theme, "You Can Fly, You Can
Fly, You Can Fly." It's *very* tame fun for the young and young at
heart. It's also another one where the long lines could inspire the
theme "you can wait, you can wait, you can wait." *Tip:* The lines
here often shrink to manageable proportions around the evening
parade times, so if you can hold out until later in the day, you
might save yourself some aggravation.

### Snow White's Scary Adventures
**Frommer's Rating:** C
**Recommended Ages:** 4–8
Though Disney has changed this ride a bit since its debut, attempt-
ing to make it less scary for the small children that it was intended
for, it still features the wicked witch rather predominantly (though
Snow White appears far more often than before). Many of the

scenes are now more pleasant, including such happier moments from the movie as the scenes at the wishing well and Snow White riding away with the prince to live happily ever after. There are new audio-animatronic dwarfs, and the colors have been brightened and made less menacing. Even so, this ride still has plenty of scary moments if your child is younger than 5 (and those much older likely won't even want to ride), so if the lines are long think about passing this one up.

### Shopping in Fantasyland

**Fantasy Faire** is filled with plenty of items for your little prince or princess to play with, including costumes, swords, and much more. Little girls adore **Tinker Bell's Treasures,** its wares comprising Peter Pan merchandise, costumes (Tinker Bell, Snow White, Cinderella, Pocahontas, and others), and collector dolls. **Pooh's Thotful Shop** is filled with T-shirts and toys featuring those cuddly characters from the Hundred-Acre Wood for kids and adults alike.

## MICKEY'S TOONTOWN FAIR

Wondering where to find Mickey? Instead of walking about the park as he did many years ago, the Mouse now holds court in Toontown. The candy-striped **Judge's** and **Toontown Hall of Fame** tents inside this zone are where kids get a chance to meet many of their favorite Disney characters, including Mickey, Minnie, Donald, Goofy, and Pluto. The entire area (small as it may be) is filled with a whimsical collection of cartoonish attractions geared mostly to those younger than 6.

*Note:* At press time, Toontown was scheduled to close due to the ongoing expansion of Fantasyland. In the meantime, the Toontown character meet-and-greets have been relocated to the Town Square Exposition Hall on Main Street, U.S.A.

### The Barnstormer at Goofy's Wiseacre Farm (Finds)

**Frommer's Rating:** A for kids and parents
**Recommended Ages:** 4 and up
Designed to look and feel like a crop duster that flies slightly off course and right through the Goofmeister's barn, this mini roller coaster is one of the more whimsically themed rides in the park. As

coasters go, it offers very little in the dip-and-drop department, but there's plenty of zip on the spin-and-spiral front. It even gets squeals from some adults. The only ones likely to be disappointed are those who live for the thrills and spills of the bigger coasters. *Note:* The 60-second ride has a 35-inch height minimum, and expectant mothers are warned not to ride it.

### Donald's Boat (S.S. *Miss Daisy*)

**Frommer's Rating:** B+ for kids
**Recommended Ages:** 2–10

The good ship *Miss Daisy* offers plenty of interactive fun for kids who enjoy getting wet. Watch out as you make your way around the surrounding "waters" as the leaks squirting from the boat are practically unavoidable—but that's half the fun (you can tell by the little squeals of joy heard from those who've been doused). *Tip:* The nearby Toon Park (a 40-in. height *maximum*) is a small covered playground with slides and a small playhouse for drier adventures.

### Mickey's & Minnie's Country Houses

**Frommer's Rating:** B for younger kids
**Recommended Ages:** 2–8

These separate cottages offer a lot of visual fun and a small bit of interactive play for youngsters, but they're usually crowded—the lines flow like molasses. Mickey's place is more for looking than touching, though it does feature a small garden and garage playground. Minnie's lets kids play in her kitchen, where popcorn goes wild in a microwave, a cake bakes and then deflates in the oven, and the utensils strike up a symphony of their own.

## Shopping in Mickey's Toontown Fair

The **Toontown Hall of Fame Tent** has continuous meetings with Disney characters, as well as a large assortment of Disney souvenirs.

# TOMORROWLAND

This land was originally designed to focus on the future, but in 1994, the WDW folks decided Tomorrowland (originally designed in the 1970s) was beginning to look a lot like "Yesteryear." So it

## (Value) Extra Magic—Extra Time

The free **Extra Magic Hour** program allows Disney resort guests (as well as those staying at the WDW Swan, the WDW Dolphin, and the Hilton at the Walt Disney World Resort) some extra playtime in the parks (even the water parks). Under the program, a select number of attractions, shops, and restaurants at one of the four major Disney parks (or one of its two water parks) open an hour early on scheduled mornings, and those at another park remain open up to 3 hours after official closing on scheduled evenings. And because only resort guests can participate in the Extra Magic Hour, crowds are almost nonexistent, and lines are much shorter—not to mention that the temperatures are usually a lot more agreeable early in the morning and later in the evening.

To enter a park for the morning Extra Magic Hour, you must present your Disney resort room key and park ticket. For the evening Extra Magic Hour, your room key, park ticket, and a special wristband (for every member in your group) are required. You can obtain the wristband at the park scheduled to remain open that evening, but no earlier than 1 hour prior to park closing.

*Warning:* If you hold a ticket with a Park Hopper add-on (see p. 102 for information on Disney ticketing options), you can attend any Extra Magic Hour at any park. But, if you hold a Base Ticket with no park-hopping privileges, you can only attend the Extra Magic Hour at the park where you're spending your day. So, if you have only a Base Ticket and go to the morning Magic Hour at Epcot and spend the day there, you cannot head over to Magic Kingdom's evening Magic Hour on the same day. Call (C) 407/824-4321 or visit www.disneyworld.com for details.

was revamped to show the future as envisioned in the 2020s and '30s—a galactic, science fiction–inspired community inhabited by humans, aliens, and robots. A video-game arcade also was added.

### Astro Orbiter

**Frommer's Rating:** C+

**Recommended Ages:** 4–10

Although touted as a tame ride much like the ones you might have ridden when you were a child and the carnivals came to town, it does offer a bit of unexpected uneasiness. Its "rockets" are on arms attached to "the center of the galaxy," and move up and down while orbiting the planets, but they also tilt to the side—and when you're on top of a two-story tower, looking down from your perch can make you rather anxious. Because of its limited capacity the line tends to move at a snail's pace, so unless it's short, skip this one.

### Buzz Lightyear's Space Ranger Spin

**Frommer's Rating:** A+ for kids and parents

**Recommended Ages:** 3 and up

Recruits stand ready as Buzz Lightyear briefs you on your mission. The evil emperor Zurg is once again up to no good, and Buzz needs your help to save the Universe. As you cruise through "space," you'll pass through scenes filled with brightly colored aliens, most of whom are marked with a big "Z," so you know where to shoot. Kids love using the dashboard-mounted laser cannons as they spin through the sky (filled with gigantic toys instead of stars). If they're good shots, they can set off sight and sound gags with a direct hit from their lasers (my 4-year-old, however, aims just about everywhere but at the target and still has loads of fun). A display in the car keeps score, so take multiple cars if you have more than one child.

### Monsters, Inc. Laugh Floor

**Frommer's Rating:** B+

**Recommended Ages:** 4 and up

Taking its cue from the hit Disney/Pixar flick *Monsters, Inc.,* Mike, along with an entire cast of monster comedians, pokes fun at audience members in hopes of getting enough laughs to fill the gigantic laugh canister. This new immersive experience is live and unscripted, using real-time animation, digital projection, sophisticated voice-activated animation, and a tremendous cast of talented improv comedians. Text message your favorite jokes to the show from your cellphone (just prior to showtimes)—and you may find yourself laughing at a joke or two of your own! The number is available near the attraction's entrance (and works only within a very short radius).

## Space Mountain

**Frommer's Rating:** B+

**Recommended Ages:** 10–adult

This cosmic roller coaster usually has *long* lines, but it has FAST-PASS. Disney has added 87 high-tech video-game stations (each themed around space travel) and updated the special effects (space-age music and exhibits—think meteorites, shooting stars, and space debris whizzing past overhead) throughout the queue in an effort to revive the coaster's futuristic appeal. Once aboard your rocket, you'll climb and dive through the inky, starlit blackness of outer space. The hairpin turns and plunges make it seem as if you're going at breakneck speed, but your car doesn't go any faster than 28 mph. While no longer outdated when compared to the newer rides out there, it is a good coming-of-age test for future thrill-ride junkies; so if your kids are just starting out on the coasters, and don't mind a spin in the dark, this is a good place to begin. *Note:* Riders must be at least 44 inches tall. Also, expectant moms and people prone to motion sickness or those with heart, neck, or back problems shouldn't climb aboard.

## Stitch's Great Escape

**Frommer's Rating:** D

**Recommended Ages:** 6–10

In 2003, the scarier **ExtraTERRORestrial Alien Encounter** was closed permanently to make way for this newer and (allegedly) more family-friendly attraction. Unfortunately, Disney missed the mark on this one. Even though it features the mischievous experiment 626, otherwise known as Stitch—a favorite of many younger kids—the ride isn't really that child-friendly (at least not for the young set). It's not particularly exciting, either. Upon entering the

**Tips** **Snacking in the Parks**

For my money, you can't beat the smoked turkey drum-sticks sold for about $6 in WDW parks (they're called "Galactic Gobblers" at the Lunching Pad in Tomorrowland). How popular are they? Each year, Disney guests gobble-gobble 1.6 million of them.

attraction, guests are briefed on their responsibilities as newly recruited alien prison guards. Suddenly an alarm sounds—a new prisoner is arriving and the pandemonium begins. Stitch, after appearing by teleportation, is confined in the middle of the room, but only momentarily—the ride isn't called Stitch's Great Escape for nothing. Guests are seated around the center stage, overhead restraints on their shoulders (which are slightly uncomfortable unless you were sitting straight up when they are lowered) allowing them to "feel" special sensory effects. It's the attraction's long peri-ods of darkness and silence that make this one inappropriate for younger children—a fact made apparent by some of the screams you'll hear from the audience. ***Note:*** There's a 40-inch height requirement to experience the attraction, though this may change—it's already been adjusted twice since the ride first debuted.

**Tomorrowland Indy Speedway**

**Frommer's Rating:** B+ for kids; D for tweens, teens, and childless adults

**Recommended Ages:** 4–10

Younger kids love this ride, especially if they get the chance to drive one of the gas-powered, minisports cars—though they may need the help of a parent's foot to push down on the gas pedal—for a 4-minute spin around the track. Tweens and teens, however, hate it: Speeds reach a mere 7 mph, which for most is *incredibly* slow, and the steering is atrocious (you can't control the cars without bumping the rail that it follows). The slow speed seems to work

**Moments** **Where to Find Characters**

**Mickey's Toontown Fair** was designed as a place where kids can meet and mingle with their favorite characters all day at the Judge's Tent and Toontown Hall of Fame Tent. Mickey, Minnie, Tinker Bell, and her fairy friends as well as a slew of others can be found in residence. In **Fantasyland,** look for Ariel's Grotto and the Fantasyland Character Festival for daily greetings. **Main Street** (Town Square), **Adventureland** (at Pirates of the Caribbean and near Magic Carpets of Aladdin), and **Tomorrowland** (near the Space Ranger Spin) are other hot spots. Be sure to have your camera ready and waiting if you want to capture the moment before it's gone.

*Tip:* If you're willing to spend money to avoid waiting in a line, character meals at such restaurants as the **Crystal Palace** and **Cinderella's Royal Table** (as well as at select WDW resorts) all offer the opportunity to meet your favorite characters. Just don't forget to make Advance Reservations if you go the dining route.

*Note:* Meet-and-greets originally held in Mickey's Toontown Fair have been temporarily moved to the Town Square Exposition Hall on Main Street, U.S.A., due to ongoing construction during the Fantasyland expansion. Upon completion, all new meet-and-greet opportunities will be available in the Fantasyland Forest and throughout the entire park.

well for young kids (who also think the bumping around is fun). The long lines move even more slowly than the ride does, so be prepared to wait this one out. There's a 52-inch height minimum to take a lap without an older rider along with you. *Note:* It carries Disney's warning that expectant mothers and people with heart, neck, or back problems shouldn't climb aboard, likely because of the potential for getting bumped as you try to board or disembark.

**Frommer's Rating:** C, B+ for tired adults and toddlers
**Recommended Ages:** All ages

After making your way up a moving walkway, you'll spot the futuristic train cars that will take you on a tour of Tomorrowland from high above the ground. The engineless train runs on a track and is powered by electromagnets, creating no pollution, little noise, and using little power. Narrated by a computer guide named Horack I, TTA offers an overhead view of Tomorrowland, including a brief interior look at Space Mountain. Lines are often nonexistent as most riders are parents awaiting the return of their children from Space Mountain, or those with tired toddlers in need of a brief respite from the activity below.

## Walt Disney's Carousel of Progress (Overrated)

**Frommer's Rating:** C
**Recommended Ages:** 5–10

Only open seasonally, when crowds are at their peak, the Carousel of Progress offers more of a respite from the hustle and bustle of the crowds than it does an interesting experience. It first debuted at the 1964 World's Fair before Disney decided to include it in his collection. The ride emigrated from Disneyland to Disney World in 1975 and was refurbished to its original state a little more than 10 years ago. The entire show rotates through scenes illustrating the state of technology from the 1900s to the 1940s. Most adults find it rather boring, but kids willing to sit still for a few minutes may actually learn a thing or two.

## Shopping in Tomorrowland

**Mickey's Star Traders** is a large shop filled from top to bottom with Disneyana; it's probably the best place to shop in the Magic Kingdom after Main Street.

# PARADES, FIREWORKS & MORE

Pick up a guide map (or two) and a *Times Guide* (or three) when you enter the park. The information includes the day's **entertainment schedule,** listing all the special goings-on for the day. Included are concerts, encounters with characters, holiday events, parades, fireworks, restaurant hours, and the major happenings listed next. *Tip:* There's also an all-parks guide that includes much of the same information and is well worth picking up, too.

### Celebrate A Dream Come True Parade

**Frommer's Rating:** B

**Recommended Ages:** All ages

Floats filled with Disney characters make their way through the park and up Main Street on a daily basis. Each features a different theme ("imagination" at the heart of each); one features Pinocchio, another Snow White, even Disney's more sinister characters, including the evil queen, Maleficent, and Cruella De Vil have their place in the parade.

### Main Street Electrical Parade (Moments

**Frommer's Rating:** A

**Recommended Ages:** All ages

After a 10-year hiatus, this popular parade has once again been brought back to life (albeit only seasonally). Fanciful floats adorned with thousands of sparkling lights and a cast of colorful characters, led by none other than Disney's most popular pixie (Tinker Bell, of course), entrance onlookers of all ages as the parade makes its way along Main Street, U.S.A. While I may not remember every last detail about my first trip to Disney (in this instance, Disneyland), the Electrical Parade left a lasting impression—so you can only imagine how impressive the parade is today (some 39 years later).

### SpectroMagic (Moments

**Frommer's Rating:** A

**Recommended Ages:** All ages

In April 2001, this after-dark display returned for a second engagement at WDW, replacing the **Main Street Electrical Parade,** a Disney classic that ran from 1976 to 1991, and again from 1996 to 2001 at the Magic Kingdom. *SpectroMagic is only held on a limited number of nights.* The 20-minute parade combines fiber optics, holographic images, clouds of liquid nitrogen, old-fashioned twinkling lights, and a soundtrack featuring classic Disney tunes. It takes the electrical equivalent of seven lightning bolts (enough to power a fleet of 2,000 over-the-road trucks) to bring

*Tip:* On some nights, during busy periods, SpectroMagic runs twice. If your party consists of adults or kids old enough to stay up late, then the second running is almost always less crowded than the first. As an added benefit, catching the late parade lets you take advantage of shorter lines at the major rides during the first running.

### Wishes

**Frommer's Rating:** A+
**Recommended Ages:** All ages

Wishes, Disney's breathtaking 12-minute fireworks display replaced the old Fantasy in the Sky fireworks in October 2003. The show, narrated by Jiminy Cricket and with background music from several Disney classics, is the story of a wish coming true, and it borrows one element from the old one—Tinker Bell still flies overhead. The fireworks go off nightly during summer and holidays, and on selected nights (usually Mon and Wed–Sat) the rest of the year. See your entertainment schedule for details. Numerous good views are available, so long as you're standing on the front side of the castle—get too far off to the side or behind the display, and it loses much of its impressive and meticulously choreographed visual effect. Disney hotels close to the park (Grand Floridian, Polynesian, Contemporary, and Wilderness Lodge) also offer excellent views.

## 4 EPCOT

*Epcot* is an acronym for *Experimental Prototype Community of Tomorrow,* and it was Walt Disney's dream for a planned city. (For an idea of what he wanted, visit **www.waltopia.com**.) Alas, after his death, it became a theme park—Central Florida's second major one, which opened in 1982.

Ever growing and changing, Epcot occupies 300 vibrantly landscaped acres. If you can spare it, take a little time to stop and smell the roses on your way to and through the two major sections: **Future World** and **World Showcase.**

Epcot is so big that hiking the World Showcase end to end (1⅓ miles from the Canada pavilion on one side to Mexico on the other) can be an exhausting experience. That's why some folks are certain Epcot stands for "Every Person Comes Out Tired." Depending on how long you intend to linger at each country in World Showcase, this part of the park can be experienced in 1 day (though you can easily spend 2). Most visitors simply make a leisurely loop, working clockwise or counterclockwise from one side of the Showcase to the other.

Unlike Magic Kingdom, much of Epcot's parking lot is close to the gate. Parking sections are named for themes (Harvest, Energy, and so forth), and the aisles are numbered. While some guests are happy to walk to the gate from nearer areas, trams are available, but these days mainly to and from the outer areas.

Be sure to pick up a guide map and entertainment schedule as you enter the park. The guide uses a white **k** in a red square to note "Kidcot" stops. These play and learning stations are for the younger set and allow them to stop at various World Showcase countries, do crafts, get autographs, have their Kidcot passports stamped (these are available for purchase in most Epcot stores and make a great souvenir), and chat with cast members native to those countries. They generally open at 1pm daily.

If you plan to eat lunch or dinner here and haven't already made Advance Reservations (☎ **407/939-3463**), you can make them at the restaurants themselves or at guest relations (near Spaceship Earth)—here you'll find a board that posts which restaurants still have space (including which meal)—and those that don't. Many Epcot restaurants are described in chapter 5, "Where to Dine."

Before you get underway, check the *Times Guide* for show schedules and incorporate any shows you want to see into your itinerary.

## SERVICES & FACILITIES IN EPCOT

**ATMS**   The machines here are located at the front of the park, in Italy, and near the bridge between World Showcase and Future World.

**BABY CARE**   Epcot's Baby Care Center is by the First Aid station near the Odyssey Center in Future World. It's furnished with a

nursing room with rocking chairs. Disposable diapers are also
available at Guest Relations.

**FIRST AID**   The First Aid Center, staffed by registered nurses, is
located near the Odyssey Center in Future World.

**LOCKERS**   Attended lockers are to the west of Spaceship Earth as
you enter the park; unattended lockers are located at the International Gateway. The cost is $7 to $9 a day, plus a $5 deposit.

**LOST CHILDREN**   Lost children in Epcot are usually taken to
Earth Center or the Baby Care Center, where lost children logbooks are kept. *Children younger than 7 should wear name-tags
inside their clothing.*

**PET CARE**   Accommodations are offered at kennels just outside
the Entrance Plaza at Epcot for $13 to $23 (© **407/824-6568**).
Proof of vaccination is required. There are also four (soon to be
five) other kennels in the WDW complex. (See chapter 2 for more
details.)

**STROLLERS**   These can be rented from special stands on the east
side of the Entrance Plaza and at World Showcase's International
Gateway. The cost is $15 for a single and $31 for a double. Length-of-stay rentals are available at $13 per day for a single and $27 per
day for a double. Full payment is required up front for length-of-stay rentals. See p. 23 for tips on using a stroller at WDW.

**WHEELCHAIR RENTAL**   Rent wheelchairs inside the Entrance
Plaza to your left, to the right of ticket booths at the Gift Shop, and
at World Showcase's International Gateway. The cost for regular
chairs is $12. Electric wheelchairs cost $50 a day, plus a $20
refundable deposit.

## FUTURE WORLD

Future World is in the northern section of Epcot, the first area
mainstream guests see after entering the park. Its icon is a huge
geosphere known as Spaceship Earth—aka, that giant golf ball.
Major corporations sponsor Future World's 10 themed areas (that
means they're making pricey investments, such as the $100 million
that Hewlett-Packard dropped on the Mission: Space ride you'll

**Moments**   **Behind the Scenes: Special Tours in Walt Disney World**

In addition to the greenhouse tour in Epcot's the Land pavilion (p. 143), the Disney parks offer a number of walking tours and learning programs. These tours, which are subject to change, represent a sampling of the most recent ones available at press time. Times, days, and prices also change. It's best to call ahead to Disney's tour line, © **407/ 939-8687,** to make reservations or get additional information. *Tip:* **Custom Guided Tours** (© **407/560-4033**) are available at $175 per hour with a 6-hour minimum.

- Epcot's **Aqua Seas Tour** lends you a wet suit and then takes you on a 2½-hour journey that includes a 30-minute swim in the 5.7-million gallon Seas with Nemo & Friends Aquarium, home to some 65 marine species. The tour includes a souvenir T-shirt, refreshments, and group photo. The cost is $140, park admission is not required, and it's open to guests 8 and older (those younger than 11 must be accompanied by a participating adult). It's offered daily at 12:30pm.

- The **Family Magic Tour** explores the nooks and crannies of the Magic Kingdom in the form of a 2-hour scavenger hunt. You meet and greet characters at the end. Children (ages 3 and older) and adults pay $34 per person. You must also buy admission tickets to the park and book in advance. If you have young kids and want to do a special tour, this is the one to take. It begins daily at 10am outside City Hall.

The following tours are for those 16 and older:

- At the top of the price chain ($224 per person) is **Backstage Magic,** a 7-hour, self-propelled bus tour through areas of Epcot, the Magic Kingdom, and Disney's Hollywood Studios that aren't seen by mainstream guests. The 10am tour (Mon–Fri only) is limited to 20 adults, and you might have trouble getting a date unless you book early. You'll see WDW mechanics and engineers repairing and building animatronic beings from it's a small world and other attractions. You'll peek over the shoulders of cast members who watch closed-circuit TVs to make sure other visitors are surviving the harrowing rides. And at the Magic Kingdom, you'll venture into the tunnels used for work areas as well as corridors for the cast to get from one area to the others without fighting tourist crowds. It's not unusual for tour takers to see Snow White enjoying a Snickers bar, find Cinderella having her locks touched up at an underground salon, or view woodworkers as they restore the hard maple muscles of the carousel horses. Park admission *isn't* required. Lunch is included.

- **Backstage Safari** at Animal Kingdom ($72 per person, plus park admission) offers a 3-hour look at the park's veterinary hospital as well as lessons in conservation, animal nutrition, and medicine (Mon and Wed–Fri). *Note:* You won't see many animals.
- **Yuletide Fantasy,** available from November 30 to December 24 (Mon–Sat) each year, gives visitors a 3½-hour front-row look at how Disney creates a winter wonderland to get visitors in the holiday spirit. It costs $84 per person, and theme-park admission *isn't* required.

read about a little later in this chapter). The focus here is on discovery, scientific achievements, and tomorrow's technologies in areas running from energy to undersea exploration.

## Imagination

**Frommer's Rating:** B+

**Recommended Ages:** 6–adult

In this pavilion, even the fountains are magical. "Water snakes" arc in the air, offering kids a chance to dare them to "bite." This pavilion was upgraded in 2001 to include more high-tech gadgets, and a year later Figment, the pavilion's much-loved mascot, returned (see below).

The 3-D **Honey, I Shrunk the Audience** ride is the big attraction here, deserving of an **"A" rating** by itself. Based on the Disney hit film *Honey, I Shrunk the Kids,* you're terrorized by mice and, once you're shrunk, by a large cat; then you're given a good shaking by a gigantic 5-year-old. Vibrating seats and creepy tactile effects enhance dramatic 3-D action. Finally, everyone returns to proper size—except the family dog, which creates the final surprise. *Note:* At press time, Honey, I Shrunk the Audience had been temporarily replaced by **Captain EO,** a futuristic 3-D flick starring Michael Jackson, first shown some 24 years ago (1986–94). Brought back by popular demand (in the wake of Jackson's untimely death), this musical adventure through space (the special effects tweaked a bit to bring it up to date) makes a surprisingly appropriate addition to Epcot's lineup of techy attractions.

**Figment,** the crazy but lovable dragon mascot of the park when it opened, was resurrected in the **Journey into Your Imagination** ride in June 2002. Things begin with an open house at the Imagination Institute, with Dr. Nigel Channing taking you on a tour of labs that demonstrate how the five senses capture and control one's imagination, except you never get to touch and taste once Figment arrives to prove it's far, far better to set your imagination free. He invites you to his upside-down house, where a new perspective enhances your imagination

Once you disembark from the ride, head for the **"What If"** labs, where your kids can burn lots of energy while exercising their imaginations at a number of interactive stations that allow them to conduct music and experiment with video.

### Innoventions East and West

**Frommer's Rating:** B+ for hungry minds and game junkies
**Recommended Ages:** 8–adult

Innoventions East, behind Spaceship Earth and to the left as you enter the park, features the Sum of All Thrills, where budding Imagineers can create (and ride) their own simulated coaster, while **Don't Waste It** is filled with edu-taining games about garbage—and how we can reduce what we produce. Across the plaza at Innoventions West, crowds flock to Video Games of Tomorrow, which has nearly three dozen game stations. **Where's the Fire,** geared to smaller kids, teaches the basics of fire safety and demonstrates how firefighters fight fires with the help of a pump truck. At **Storm Struck,** the focus is on wild weather, as hurricanes, tornados, and other storms are explored in 3-D.

*Note:* The Underwriters Laboratories exhibit at Innoventions East, the **Test the Limits Lab,** has six kiosks that let kids and fun-loving adults try out a variety of products.

### The Land

**Frommer's Rating:** B+ for environmentalists, gardeners; C+ for others
**Recommended Ages:** 8–adult

The largest of Future World's pavilions highlights food and nature. **Living with the Land** is a 13-minute boat ride through three ecological environments (a rainforest, an African desert, and the windswept American plains), each populated by appropriate audio-animatronic denizens. New farming methods and experiments ranging from hydroponics to plants growing in simulated Martian soil are showcased in real gardens. If you'd like a more serious overview, take the 45-minute **Behind the Seeds** guided walking tour of the growing areas, offered daily. Sign up at the Green Thumb Emporium shop on the ground floor near the Sunshine Season Food Festival. The cost is $16 for adults, $12 for children 3 to 9. *Note:* It's really geared to children.

**Circle of Life** combines spectacular live-action footage with animation in a 15-minute motion picture based on *The Lion King.*

In this cautionary environmental tale, Timon and Pumbaa are building a monument to the good life called Hakuna Matata Lakeside Village, but their project, as Simba points out, is damaging the savanna for other animals. The message: Everything is connected in the great circle of life.

**Soarin'** is a copy of a popular attraction at Disney's California Adventure theme park. Guests are seated in giant hang gliders and surrounded by a tremendous projection-screen dome. After being lifted up more than 40 feet into the air, you'll fly through the sky over the landscapes of California. This amazing adventure is enhanced by sensory effects as guests are treated to the sights, sounds . . . and smells (think orange blossoms and pine trees) of a dozen locations in California, including the Golden Gate Bridge, the redwood forests, Napa Valley, Yosemite, and more. You really will feel almost as if you're flying through the sky. The ride carries a 40-inch height minimum.

## Mission: Space

**Frommer's Rating:** A+

**Recommended Ages:** 10–adult

This $100-million attraction, developed in partnership with Hewlett-Packard and NASA, seats up to four riders at a time in a simulated flight to the Red Planet. You'll assume the role of commander, pilot, navigator, or engineer, depending on where you sit, and must complete related jobs vital to the mission (don't worry if you miss your cue, you won't crash). The ride uses a combination of visuals, sound, and centrifugal force to create the illusion of a launch and trip to Mars. Even veteran roller-coaster riders who tried the simulator said the sensation mimics a liftoff, as riders are pressed into their seats and the roar and vibration tricks the brain during the launch portion of the 4-minute adventure. As one of only two real thrillers in the park, this one often has incredibly long lines, so get here early or FASTPASS it. A second less-intense version of the ride is available, the spinning sensation removed altogether. The original, or orange, version is definitely not for the faint at heart—the green, however, is far less intense and allows astronauts-in-training (those not ready for G-forces and spinning simulators) the chance to experience space. ***Note:*** Riders must be at least 44 inches tall. If you're claustrophobic, have a low tolerance for loud noises,

> ### (Kids) Where's Mickey?
>
> Although I've mentioned on more than one occasion that
> Epcot is the least tot-friendly of the Disney parks, I have to
> admit, Disney's made a concerted effort to change (or at
> least better) its image. Rides and attractions have been
> revamped (becoming far more kid-friendly), Kidcot stations
> can now be found at almost every World Showcase pavil-
> ion (there are even a few in Future World), and characters
> walk the park on a daily basis—there's even a new indoor
> meet-and-greet spot (aptly named the Character Connec-
> tion) located next to the Fountainview Café, and a new
> interactive super-spy secret-agent-style adventure (Disney's
> Kim Possible World Showcase Adventure) has been added.
> For the preschool set, kid-friendly maps (that include all the
> Disney parks—even the water parks) are available at guest
> relations.

or have stuffy sinuses, then you should avoid the ride all together.
If spinning causes you to get dizzy or motion sick, simply avoid the
orange version and head directly for the line marked in green.

### The Seas with Nemo & Friends
**Frommer's Rating:** B+
**Recommended Ages:** 3–adult
This newly transformed pavilion is still home to a signature
aquarium filled with 5.7-million-gallons of saltwater and coral
reefs inhabited by some 4,000 sharks, barracudas, parrotfish, rays,
dolphins, and other critters. Now, however, instead of exhibits trac-
ing the history of undersea exploration and a 7-minute edu-flick,
you'll pass through a serene undersea setting before climbing
aboard a "clamobile" to ride **The Seas with Nemo & Friends.**
Guests join in on an undersea field trip led by Mr. Ray, who even-
tually discovers that Nemo's gone missing and it's up to everyone
to find him. This family-friendly ride slowly moves riders past

several stunning undersea scenes in search of everyone's favorite clownfish. Thanks to new animation technology, Marlin, Dory, Mr. Ray, Bruce, and other familiar finned friends seemingly swim right along with the live inhabitants of the aquarium. Be sure to check out the adorable **Turtle Talk with Crush.** Crush (from *Finding Nemo*) chitchats with the audience from behind his undersea movie screen, engaging them in conversation and telling a joke or two. This is a first-of-its-kind attraction using digital projection and voice-activated animation to create a real-time experience. Your kids will get a huge kick out of it; you will, too.

**Bruce's Shark World,** a small interactive play area, is the perfect spot to let little ones run around, climb, and work off excess energy—not to mention snap a photo or two.

*Note:* The **Epcot DiveQuest** enables certified divers (ages 10–14 must have a scuba-certified adult accompany them, ages 10–17 must have a signed parental waiver) to participate in a 3-hour program that includes a 40-minute dive in the Living Seas aquarium. The program costs $175 (Tues-Sat). Call ✆ **407/939-8687** for more information.

> **Moments**  **Water Fountain Conversations**
>
> Many an ordinary item at Disney World has hidden entertainment value. Take a drink at the water fountain in Innoventions Plaza (the one right next to MouseGear) and it may beg you not to drink it dry. No, you haven't gotten too much sun—the fountain actually talks (much to the delight of kids and the surprise of unsuspecting adults). A few more talking fountains are scattered around Epcot. The fountains aren't the only items at WDW that talk. I've kibitzed with a walking and talking garbage can (named PUSH) in Magic Kingdom, and a personable palm tree (who goes by Wes Palm) at Animal Kingdom. Ask a Disney employee to direct you if you want to meet one of these chatty contraptions.

## Spaceship Earth (Overrated)

**Frommer's Rating:** C

**Recommended Ages:** All ages

This massive, silvery geosphere symbolizes Epcot and is probably the most recognizable Disney icon next to Cinderella Castle. That makes it a must-do for many, though it's something of a yawner for others. The 15-minute show/ride takes visitors to the distant past where an audio-animatronic Cro-Magnon shaman recounts the story of a hunt while others record it on cave walls. You advance thousands of years to ancient Egypt, where hieroglyphics adorn temple walls. You'll progress through the Phoenician and Greek alphabets, the Gutenberg printing press, and the Renaissance. Technologies develop at a rapid pace, through the telegraph, telephone, radio, movies, and TV. Then it's on to the age of electronic communications before catapulting into outer space. While the premise remains the same, recent (and long overdue) updates have brought this adventure through time more in line with the park's other edutaining offerings. Judi Dench now narrates as you move slowly along the track. Touch screens add an interactive element. **"Project Tomorrow: Inventing the World of Tomorrow"** is a hands-on post-show exhibit filled with futuristic games focusing on such themes as medicine, transportation, and energy management.

## Test Track

**Frommer's Rating:** A+

**Recommended Ages:** 8–adult

Test Track is a $60-million marvel that combines GM engineering and Disney Imagineering. The line can be more than an hour long in peak periods, so consider the FASTPASS option (but remember to get one early before they run out). The last part of the line snakes through displays about corrosion, crash tests, and other things from the GM proving grounds (you can linger long enough to see them even with FASTPASS). The 5-minute ride follows what looks to be an actual highway. It includes braking tests, a hill climb, and tight S-curves in a six-passenger convertible. The left front seat offers the most thrills as the vehicle moves through the curves. There's also a 12-second burst of speed that reaches 65 mph on the straightaway (no traffic!). *Note:* Riders must be at least 40 inches tall. Also, expectant mothers and people prone to motion sickness or those with heart, neck, or back problems shouldn't test the track.

*Note II:* This is the only attraction in Epcot that has a single-rider line, which allows singles to fill in vacant spots in select cars. If you're part of a party that doesn't mind splitting up and riding in singles, you can shave off some serious waiting time by taking advantage of this option.

*Note III:* Test Track often experiences technical difficulties and, to add insult to injury, it's one of the few rides in Epcot that closes due to inclement weather. If you know a storm's brewing in the afternoon, be sure to head here early in the day.

## Universe of Energy

**Frommer's Rating:** B+

**Recommended Ages:** 6–adult

Sponsored by Exxon, this pavilion has a roof full of solar panels and a goal of bettering your understanding of America's energy problems and potential solutions. Its 32-minute ride, **Ellen's Energy Adventure,** features comedian Ellen DeGeneres being tutored (by Bill Nye the Science Guy) to be a *Jeopardy!* contestant. On a massive screen in Theater I, an animated motion picture depicts the earth's molten beginnings, its cooling process, and the formation of fossil fuels. You move back in time 275 million years into an eerie, storm-wracked landscape of the Mesozoic Era, a time of violent geological activity. Here, giant audio-animatronic dragonflies, earthquakes, and streams of molten lava threaten you before you enter a steam-filled tunnel deep in the bowels of a volcano. When you emerge, you're in Theater II and the present. In this new setting, which looks like a NASA Mission Control room, a 70mm film projected on a massive 210-foot wraparound screen depicts the challenges of the world's increasing energy demands and the emerging technologies that will help meet them. Your moving seats now return to Theater I, where swirling special effects herald a film about how energy impacts our lives. It ends on an upbeat note, with a vision of an energy-abundant future, and Ellen as a new *Jeopardy!* champion. *Note:* I've taken kids as young as 2 on this ride with no problems, but recommend that children be at least 6 or they won't get much out of the experience beyond flashing lights and sounds.

## Shopping in Future World

Most of Epcot's more unique shopping lies just ahead in World Showcase, but there are a few places in this part of the park that offer special souvenirs. You can browse through cels and other collectibles at the **Art of Disney** in Innoventions West (how about an $8,800, 5-ft. wooden Mickey watch?), purchase almost anything imaginable at **MouseGear** in Innovations East (one of the best and most comprehensive shops in all of WDW) in Innoventions East, and find gardening and other gifts in the **Land.**

## WORLD SHOWCASE

You can tour the world in a day at this community of 11 miniaturized nations, which line the 40-acre World Showcase Lagoon on the park's southern side. All of the showcase's countries have authentically indigenous architecture, landscaping, background music, restaurants, and shops. The nations' cultural facets are explored in art exhibits, song and dance performances, and innovative rides, films, and attractions. And all of the employees in each pavilion are natives of the country represented.

All pavilions offer some kind of live entertainment throughout the day. Times and performances change, but they're listed in the guide map and on the *Times Guide.* World Showcase opens between 11am and noon daily, so there's time for a Future World excursion if you arrive earlier. *Note:* There are **regular appearances by characters** at Showcase Plaza (consult the daily schedule for times).

### Canada

**Frommer's Rating:** A
**Recommended Ages:** 8–adult
Our neighbors to the north are represented by architecture ranging from a mansard-roofed replica of Ottawa's 19th-century French–style Château Laurier (here called Hôtel du Canada) to a British-influenced stone building modeled after a famous landmark near Niagara Falls.

An Indian village, complete with a rough-hewn log trading post and 30-foot replicas of Ojibwa totem poles, signifies the culture of the Northwest. The Canadian wilderness is reflected by a rocky mountain; a waterfall cascading into a white-water stream; and a miniforest of evergreens, stately cedars, maples, and birch trees. Don't miss the stunning floral displays of azaleas, roses, zinnias, chrysanthemums, petunias, and patches of wildflowers inspired by the Butchart Gardens just outside of Victoria, British Columbia.

The pavilion's highlight attraction is *O Canada!*—a dazzling (and recently updated) 18-minute, 360-degree CircleVision film that shows Canada's scenic splendor, from a dogsled race to its modern cities and diverse people. If you're looking for foot-tapping live entertainment, **Off Kilter** raises the roof with New Age Celtic music as well as some get-down country music. Days and times vary.

**Northwest Mercantile** carries sandstone carvings, fringed leather vests, duck decoys, moccasins, Native American dolls, rabbit-skin caps, heavy knitted sweaters, and, of course, maple syrup.

## China

**Frommer's Rating:** A
**Recommended Ages:** 10–adult

Bounded by a serpentine wall that snakes around its perimeter, the China pavilion is entered via a triple-arched ceremonial gate inspired by the Temple of Heaven in Beijing, a summer retreat for Chinese emperors. Passing through the gate, you'll see a half-size replica of this ornately embellished red-and-gold circular temple, built in 1420 during the Ming dynasty. Chinese tomb sculptures, similar to those recently unearthed near Xian, China, were recently added. Gardens simulate those in Suzhou, with miniature waterfalls, fragrant lotus ponds, and groves of bamboo, corkscrew willows, and weeping mulberry trees.

*Reflections of China* ★★ is a 20-minute movie that explores the culture and landscapes in and around Hong Kong, Beijing, Shanghai, and the Great Wall (begun 24 c. ago!), among other places. **Land of Many Faces** is an exhibit that introduces China's ethnic peoples, and entertainment is provided daily by the amazing **Dragon Legend Acrobats** ★★.

The **Yong Feng Shangdian Shopping Gallery** features silk robes, lacquer and inlaid mother-of-pearl furniture, jade figures, cloisonné vases, Yixing teapots, brocade pajamas, silk rugs and embroideries, wind chimes, and Chinese clothing. Artisans occasionally demonstrate calligraphy.

## France

**Frommer's Rating:** B

**Recommended Ages:** 8–adult

This pavilion focuses on La Belle Epoque, a period from 1870 to 1910 in which French art, literature, and architecture flourished. It's entered via a replica of the beautiful cast-iron Pont des Arts footbridge over the Seine. It leads to a park with bleached sycamores, Bradford pear trees, flowering crape myrtle, and sculptured parterre flower gardens inspired by Seurat's painting *A Sunday Afternoon on the Island of La Grande Jatte.* A one-tenth-scale replica of the Eiffel Tower constructed from Gustave Eiffel's original blueprints looms above *les grands boulevards.*

The highlight is *Impressions de France.* Shown in a palatial sit-down theater a la Fontainebleau, this 18-minute film is a scenic journey through diverse French landscapes projected on a vast 200-degree wraparound screen and enhanced by the music of French composers. The antics of **Serveur Amusant,** a comedic waiter, delight children and adults, as do the yummy pastries at **Boulangerie Patisserie.**

The covered arcade has shops selling French prints and original art, cookbooks, wines (there's a tasting counter), French food, Babar books, perfumes, and original letters of famous Frenchmen ranging from Jean Cocteau to Napoleon.

## Germany

**Frommer's Rating:** B

**Recommended Ages:** 8–adult

Enclosed by castle walls and towers, this festive pavilion is centered on a cobblestone *platz* (square) with pots of colorful flowers girding a fountain statue of St. George and the Dragon. An adjacent clock tower is embellished with whimsical glockenspiel figures that herald each hour with quaint melodies. The pavilion's **Biergarten**

## (Finds) **Great Things to Buy at Epcot**

Sure, *you* want to be educated about the cultures of the world, but for most, the two big attractions at the World Showcase are eating and shopping. Dining options are explained in chapter 5. This list gives you an idea of additional items available for purchase.

- The silver jewelry at the Mexico pavilion is beautiful. Choose from a range of merchandise, from a simple flowered hair clip to a kidney-shaped stone-and-silver bracelet. The outdoor outpost is filled top to bottom with Mexico's national soccer team merchandise.

- There are lots of great sweaters available in the shops of Norway, and it's really tough to resist the Scandinavian trolls. They're so ugly, you have to love them.

- Forget about all those knockoff products stamped "Made in China." The merchandise in this country is among the more expensive to be found in Epcot, from jade teardrop earrings to multicolored bracelets to Disney art.

- Porcelain and cuckoo clocks are the things to look at in Germany. You might find a Goebel Collectible Winnie the Pooh or a handcrafted Pooh cuckoo clock. Of course, Hümmel figurines and stuffed Steiffs are big sellers, too.

- In Italy, look for 100% silk scarves in a variety of patterns as well as fine silk ties and crystal.

- Your funky teenager might like the Taquia knit cap, a colorful fezlike chapeau, that's available in Morocco. There's also a variety of celestial-patterned pottery available in vases and platters.

- Tennis fans may be interested in the Wimbledon shirts, shorts, and skirts available in the United Kingdom. There's also a nice assortment of rose-patterned tea accessories, Shetland sweaters, and pub accessories.

was inspired by medieval Rothenberg and features a year-round Oktoberfest and its music. And 16th-century facades replicate a merchant's hall in the Black Forest and the town hall in Römerberg Square.

The shops here carry Hümmel figurines, crystal, glassware, cookware, Anton Schneider cuckoos, cowbells, Alpine hats, German wines (there's a tasting counter), specialty foods, toys (German Disneyana, teddy bears, dolls, and puppets), and books. An artisan demonstrates molding and painting Hümmel figures; another paints detailed scenes on eggs. Background music runs from oompah bands to Mozart symphonies.

### Italy

**Frommer's Rating:** B
**Recommended Ages:** 10–adult

One of the prettiest World Showcase pavilions, Italy lures visitors over an arched stone footbridge to a replica of Venice's intricately ornamented pink-and-white Doge's Palace. Other architectural highlights include the 83-foot Campanile (bell tower) of St. Mark's Square, Venetian bridges, and a piazza enclosing a version of Bernini's Neptune Fountain. A garden wall suggests a backdrop of provincial countryside, and citrus, cypress, pine, and olive trees frame a formal garden. Gondolas are moored on the lagoon.

Shops carry cameo and filigree jewelry, Armani figurines, kitchenware, Italian wines and foods, Murano and other Venetian glass, alabaster figurines, and inlaid wooden music boxes.

In the street entertainment department, the World Showcase Players, a talented group of actors, can often be seen performing skits in the pavilions courtyard.

### Japan

**Frommer's Rating:** A
**Recommended Ages:** 8–adult

A flaming red *torii* (gate of honor) on the banks of the lagoon and the graceful blue-roofed Goju No To pagoda, inspired by a shrine built at Nara in A.D. 700, welcome you to this pavilion, which focuses on Japan's ancient culture. In a traditional Japanese garden, cedars, yews, bamboo, "cloud-pruned" evergreens, willows, and flowering shrubs frame a contemplative setting of pebbled footpaths, rustic bridges, waterfalls, exquisite rock landscaping, and a pond of golden koi. It's a haven of tranquillity in a park that's anything but. The **Yakitori House** is based on the renowned 16th-century Katsura Imperial Villa in Kyoto, designed as a royal summer residence and considered by many to be the crowning achievement of Japanese architecture. The moated **White Heron Castle** is a replica of the Shirasagi-Jo, a 17th-century fortress overlooking the city of Himeji. The **Bijutsu-kan Gallery** displays changing exhibits on various aspects of Japanese culture (for example, a past exhibit focused on Japanese tin toys).

The **Mitsukoshi Department Store** (Japan's answer to Macy's) is housed in a replica of the Shishinden (Hall of Ceremonies) of the Gosho Imperial Palace, built in Kyoto in A.D. 794. It sells lacquerware, kimonos, kites, fans, dolls in traditional costumes, origami books, samurai swords, Japanese Disneyana, bonsai trees, Japanese foods, Netsuke carvings, pottery, and modern electronics.

The drums of **Matsuriza**—one of the best performances in the World Showcase—entertain guests daily.

### Mexico

**Frommer's Rating:** A

**Recommended Ages:** 8–adult

You'll hear the music of marimbas and mariachi bands as you approach the festive showcase of Mexico, fronted by a towering pyramid modeled on the Aztec temple of Quetzalcoatl (God of Life) and surrounded by dense Yucatán jungle landscaping. Upon entering the pavilion, you'll be in a museum of pre-Columbian art and artifacts.

Down a ramp, a small lagoon is the setting for the **Gran Fiesta Tour Starring the Three Caballeros,** where visitors board boats for an 8-minute cruise through Mexico. A new animated overlay (along with refurbished backdrops and sound) features José and Panchito as they search the Mexican countryside for Donald Duck before finally reuniting in Mexico City. Passengers get a close-up look at the Mayan pyramid. **Mariachi Cobre,** a 12-piece band, plays Tuesday to Saturday.

Shops in and around the **Plaza de Los Amigos** (a "moonlit" Mexican *mercado* [market] with a tiered fountain and street lamps) display an array of leather goods, baskets, sombreros, piñatas, pottery, embroidered dresses and blouses, maracas, jewelry, serapes, colorful papier-mâché birds, and blown-glass objects (an artisan occasionally gives demonstrations). The Mexican Tourist Office also provides travel information.

### Morocco

**Frommer's Rating:** A
**Recommended Ages:** 10–adult

This exotic pavilion has architecture embellished with geometrically patterned tile work, minarets, hand-painted wood ceilings, and brass lighting fixtures (the king of Morocco sent his own royal artisans to work on the pavilion). It's headlined by a replica of the Koutoubia Minaret, the prayer tower of a 12th-century mosque in Marrakesh. The Medina (old city), entered via a replica of an arched gateway in Fez, leads to **Fez House** (a traditional Moroccan home) and the narrow, winding streets of the **souk,** a bustling marketplace where all manner of authentic handcrafted merchandise is on display. Here you can browse or purchase pottery, brassware, hand-knotted Berber or colorful Rabat carpets, ornate silver and camel-bone boxes, straw baskets, and prayer rugs. There are weaving demonstrations in the souk periodically during the day. The Medina's rectangular courtyard centers on a replica of the ornately tiled Najjarine Fountain in Fez, the setting for musical entertainment.

    **Treasures of Morocco** is a three-times-per-day 45-minute guided tour (1–5pm) that highlights this country's culture, architecture, and history. The pavilion's **Gallery of Arts and History** contains an ever-changing exhibit of Moroccan art, and the Center of Tourism offers a continuous three-screen slide show. Morocco's landscaping includes a formal garden, citrus and olive trees, date palms, and banana plants. On the entertainment side, **Mo'Rockin'** plays Arabian rock music on traditional instruments daily.

### Norway

**Frommer's Rating:** B+
**Recommended Ages:** 10–adult

This pavilion is centered on a picturesque cobblestone courtyard. A *stavekirke* (stave church), styled after the 13th-century Gol Church of Hallingdal, has changing exhibits. A replica of Oslo's 14th-century **Akershus Castle,** next to a cascading woodland waterfall, is the setting for the featured restaurant (p. 97). Other buildings simulate the red-roofed cottages of Bergen and the timber-sided farm buildings of the Nordic woodlands.

There's a two-part attraction here. **Maelstrom,** a boat ride in a dragon-headed Viking vessel, traverses Norway's fjords and mythical forests to the music of *Peer Gynt.* (It's the only attraction in World Showcase that offers FASTPASS.) Along the way, you'll see images of polar bears prowling the shore, and then trolls cast a spell on the boat. The watercraft crashes through a narrow gorge and spins into the North Sea, where a storm is in progress. (This is a relatively calm ride, though it's not recommended for expectant mothers or folks with heart, neck, or back problems.) The storm abates, and passengers disembark safely to a 10th-century Viking village to view the 5-minute 70mm film *Norway,* which documents 1,000 years of history. **Spelmanns Gledje** entertains with Norwegian folk music.

Shops sell hand-knit wool hats and authentic (and expensive) Scandinavian sweaters, troll dolls, toys (there's a LEGO table where kids can play), woodcarvings, Scandinavian foods, pewterware, and jewelry.

### United Kingdom

**Frommer's Rating:** B

**Recommended Ages:** 8–adult

The U.K. pavilion takes you to Merry Olde England through **Britannia Square,** a formal London-style park complete with a copper-roof gazebo bandstand, a stereotypical red phone booth, and a statue of the Bard. Four centuries of architecture are represented along quaint cobblestone streets; there's a traditional British pub; and a formal garden with low box hedges in geometric patterns, flagstone paths, and a stone fountain that replicates the landscaping of 16th- and 17th-century palaces.

The **British Invasion,** a group that impersonates the Beatles (Mon-Sat), and pub performers (Tues, Thurs, Fri, and Sun) provide entertainment. High Street and Tudor Lane shops display a broad sampling of British merchandise, including toy soldiers, Paddington bears, personalized coats of arms, Scottish clothing (cashmere and Shetland sweaters, golf wear, tams, and tartans), English china, Waterford crystal, and pub items such as tankards, dartboards, and the like. A tea shop occupies a replica of Anne Hathaway's thatched-roof 16th-century cottage in Stratford-on-Avon. Other emporia represent the Georgian, Victorian, Queen Anne, and Tudor periods.

### U.S.A.—The American Adventure

**Frommer's Rating:** A

**Recommended Ages:** 8–adult

Housed in a vast Georgian-style structure, the **American Adventure** is a 29-minute dramatization of U.S. history, utilizing a 72-foot rear-projection screen, rousing music, and a large cast of lifelike audio-animatronic figures, including narrators Mark Twain and Ben Franklin. The adventure begins with the voyage of the *Mayflower* and encompasses major historic events. You'll view Jefferson writing the Declaration of Independence, Matthew Brady photographing a family about to be divided by the Civil War, the stock market crash of 1929 (but not the crash of Disney stock in 1999 and 2000), Pearl Harbor, and the *Eagle* heading toward the moon. Teddy Roosevelt discusses the need for national parks. Susan B. Anthony speaks out on women's rights; Frederick Douglass, on slavery; and Chief Joseph, on the plight of Native Americans. It's one of Disney's best historical productions. Formal gardens shaded by live oaks, sycamores, elms, and holly complement the 18th-century architecture.

Entertainment includes the **Spirit of America Fife & Drum Corps,** and the **Voices of Liberty,** an a cappella group that sings patriotic songs.

**Heritage Manor Gifts** sells autographed presidential photographs, needlepoint samplers, quilts, pottery, candles, Davy Crockett hats, books on American history, historically costumed dolls, classic political campaign buttons, and vintage newspapers with banner headlines such as "Nixon Resigns!"

## OTHER SHOWS
### IllumiNations ⓒ Moments
**Frommer's Rating:** A+

**Recommended Ages:** 3–adult

Little has changed since Epcot's millennium version of IllumiNations ended on January 1, 2001. This 13-minute grand nightcap continues to be a blend of fireworks, lasers, and fountains in a display that's signature Disney. The show is worth the crowds that flock to the parking lot when it's over (just be sure to keep a firm grip on young kids). *Tip:* Stake your claim to your favorite viewing area a half-hour before show time (listed in your entertainment schedule). The ones near Showcase Plaza have a head start for the exits. Another good place for viewing the show is the terrace at the **Rose & Crown Pub** in the United Kingdom (p. 156).

# 5 DISNEY'S HOLLYWOOD STUDIOS

You'll probably see the Tower of Terror and the Earrfel Tower, a water tank with mouse ears, even before you enter this park (formerly the Disney–MGM Studios), which Disney bills as "the Hollywood that never was and always will be." Once inside, you'll find pulse-quickening rides such as **Rock 'n' Roller Coaster,** movie- and TV-themed shows such as *The Voyage of the Little Mermaid* and *The American Idol Experience,* and a spectacular laser-light show called **Fantasmic!** The main streets include Hollywood and Sunset boulevards, where Art Deco movie sets remember the golden age of Hollywood. The Streets of America sets include New York, lined with miniature renditions of Gotham's landmarks (the Empire State, Flatiron, and Chrysler buildings); as well as San Francisco, Chicago, and others. Pixar Place (formerly part of Mickey Ave.) is home to **Toy Story Mania.** You'll find some of the best street performers in the Disney parks here.

Arrive at the park early. Unlike Epcot, the Studio's 154 acres of attractions can pretty much be seen in a day. The parking lot reaches to the gate, but trams serve the outlying areas. Pay attention to your parking location; this lot isn't as well marked as the Magic Kingdom's. Again, write your lot and row number on something you'll be able to find at the end of the day.

If you don't get a *Hollywood Studios Guide Map* and entertainment schedule as you enter the park, you can pick one up at Guest Relations or most shops. First things first—check show times and then sketch out a plan for your day, because many of the of the park's best offerings are its shows. Schedule your rides around the shows that interest you most and go from there.

## SERVICES & FACILITIES IN DISNEY'S HOLLYWOOD STUDIOS

**ATMS**   ATMs are located on the right side of the main entrance and near Toy Story Pizza Planet.

**BABY CARE**   The Studios has a small Baby Care Center to the left of the main entrance where you'll find facilities for nursing and changing.

**FIRST AID**   The First Aid Center, staffed by registered nurses, is in the Entrance Plaza adjoining Guest Relations and the Baby Care Center.

**LOCKERS**   Lockers are located alongside Oscar's Classic Car Souvenirs, to the right of the Entrance Plaza after you pass through the turnstiles. The cost is $7 to $9, with an additional $5 deposit.

**LOST CHILDREN**   Lost children at Disney's Hollywood Studios are taken to Guest Relations, where lost children logbooks are kept. *Children younger than 7 should wear name-tags inside their clothes.*

**PET CARE**   Accommodations for $13 to $23 are offered at kennels to the left and just outside the entrance (*C* **407/824-6568**). There are also four other kennels in the WDW complex. (See chapter 2 for more details.) Proof of vaccinations is required.

**STROLLERS**   Strollers can be rented at Oscar's Super Service, inside the main entrance, for $15 for a single and $31 for a double.

Length-of-stay rentals are available at $13 per day for a single and $27 per day for a double. Full payment is expected up front for length-of-stay rentals.

**TIP BOARD**   The board listing the day's shows, ride closings, and other information at the corner of Hollywood and Sunset boulevards.

**WHEELCHAIR RENTAL**   Wheelchairs are rented at Oscar's Super Service inside the main entrance. The cost for regular chairs is $10 a day. Electric wheelchairs rent for $45, plus a $20 refundable deposit.

## MAJOR ATTRACTIONS & SHOWS
### American Film Institute Showcase
Frommer's Rating: C
**Recommended Ages:** 10–adult
This shop and exhibit area is the final stop on the Backlot Tour (see below) and looks at the efforts of the editors, cinematographers, producers, and directors whose names roll by in the blur of credits. It also showcases the work of the American Film Institute's Lifetime Achievement Award winners, including Bette Davis, Jack Nicholson, and Elizabeth Taylor. A special exhibit here, **"Villains: Movie Characters You Love to Hate,"** features the costumes and props of several notable bad guys, including Darth Vader.

### Beauty and the Beast Live on Stage
**Frommer's Rating:** B+
**Recommended Ages:** All ages
A 1,500-seat covered amphitheater is the home of this 30-minute live Broadway-style production of *Beauty and the Beast* that's adapted from the movie. Musical highlights from the show include the rousing "Be Our Guest" opening number and the poignant title song featured in the romantic waltz scene finale. The sets and costumes are lavish, and the production numbers are pretty spectacular. There are usually four or five shows a day.

### Disney's Hollywood Studios Backlot Tour
**Frommer's Rating:** B+
**Recommended Ages:** 6–adult

This 35-minute tram tour takes you behind the scenes for a close-up look at the vehicles, props, costumes, sets, and special effects used in your favorite movies and TV shows. On many days, you'll see costume makers at work in the wardrobe department (Disney has around two million garments here). But the real fun begins when the tram heads for **Catastrophe Canyon,** where an earthquake in the heart of oil country causes canyon walls to rumble. A raging oil fire, massive explosions, torrents of rain, and flash floods threaten you and other riders before you're taken behind the scenes to see how filmmakers use special effects to make such disasters.

### Fantasmic! Moments
**Frommer's Rating:** A+
**Recommended Ages:** All ages

Disney mixes heroes, villains, stunt performers, choreography, laser lights, and fireworks into a spectacular end-of-the-day extravaganza. This is a 25-minute visual feast where the Magic Mickey comes to life in a show featuring shooting comets, great balls of fire (my apologies to Jerry Lee), and animated fountains that really charge the audience. The cast includes 50 performers, a giant dragon, a king cobra, and 1 million gallons of water, just about all of which are orchestrated by a sorcerer mouse that looks more than remotely familiar. You'll also shudder at the animated villainy of Jafar, Cruella De Vil, and Maleficent in the battle of good vs. evil, part of which is projected onto huge, water-mist screens. The amphitheater holds 9,000 souls, including standing room, and during busy periods (holidays and summers) it's often standing-room-only, so arrive at least 30 to 60 minutes early. There is sometimes an additional show earlier in the evening. ***Note:*** The show's loud pyrotechnics may frighten younger children, and earplugs aren't a bad idea for anyone with ears sensitive to very loud noises.

### The Great Movie Ride
**Frommer's Rating:** C for most, B+ for adults who love classics
**Recommended Ages:** 8–adult

Film footage and 50 audio-animatronic replicas of movie stars are used to re-create some of the most famous scenes in filmdom on this 22-minute ride through movie history. You'll relive magic

## (Finds) Find the Hidden Mickeys

**Hidden Mickeys** started as an inside joke among early Disney Imagineers and soon became a park tradition (I'm not kidding—the entire Disney's Hollywood Studios layout when viewed from the sky is one giant Hidden Mickey!). Today, dozens of subtle Mickey images—usually silhouettes of his world-famous ears, profile, or full figure—are hidden (more or less) in attractions and resorts throughout the Walt Disney empire. No one knows how many, because sometimes they exist only in the eye of the beholder. But there's a semiofficial, maybe-you-agree-maybe-you-don't list. See how many HMs (Hidden Mickeys) you can locate during your visit. And be sharp-eyed about it. Those bubbles on your souvenir mug might be forming one. Here are a few to get you started:

### IN THE MAGIC KINGDOM

- In the Haunted Mansion banquet scene, check out the arrangement of the plate and adjoining saucers on the table.
- In the Africa scene of it's a small world, note the purple flowers on a vine on the elephant's left side.
- While riding Splash Mountain, look for Mickey lying on his back in the pink clouds to the right of the *Zip-A-Dee Lady* paddle-wheeler.

### AT EPCOT

- In Imagination, check out the little girl's dress in the lobby film of *Honey, I Shrunk the Audience,* one of five HMs in this pavilion.
- There are three HMs on the wall surrounding Mission: Space.

- As you enter the Mexico pavilion, check out the large block statue on your right as you climb the stairs—the Hidden Mickey is right at the top.
- In Maelstrom in the Norway pavilion, a Viking wears Mickey ears in the wall mural facing the loading dock.
- There are four HMs inside Spaceship Earth, one of them in the Renaissance scene, on the page of a book behind the sleeping monk. Try to find the other three.

## AT DISNEY'S HOLLYWOOD STUDIOS

- On the Great Movie Ride, there's an HM on the window above the bank in the gangster scene.
- At Jim Henson's Muppet*Vision 3-D, take a good look at the top of the sign listing five reasons for turning in your 3-D glasses, and note the balloons in the film's final scene.
- In the Twilight Zone Tower of Terror, note the bell for the elevator behind Rod Serling in the film. There are more than eight HMs in this attraction.
- Outside Rock 'n' Roller Coaster, look for two HMs in the rotunda area's tile floor. (Reportedly, the entire coaster is one giant HM.)

## IN ANIMAL KINGDOM

- Look at the Boneyard in DinoLand U.S.A., where a fan and two hard hats form an HM.
- There are 25 Hidden Mickeys at Rafiki's Planet Watch, where Mickey lurks in the murals, tree trunks, and paintings of animals.

For more information on the plethora of HMs at WDW, check out **www.hiddenmickeys.org**.

moments from the 1930s through the present: the classic airport farewell scene by Bergman and Bogart in *Casablanca;* Brando bellowing "Stellaaaaa"; Harrison Ford in full Indiana Jones mode while facing all of those snakes; Sigourney Weaver fending off slimy aliens; Gene Kelly singin' in the rain; and arguably the best Tarzan, Johnny Weissmuller, giving his trademark yell while swinging across the jungle. The action is enhanced by special effects, and outlaws hijack your tram en route. So pay attention when the conductor warns, "Fasten your seat belts. It's going to be a bumpy night." The setting is a full-scale reproduction of Hollywood's famous Mann's Chinese Theatre, complete with handprints of the stars out front. *Note:* Though it's a classic, the ride is somewhat dated and is often the target of rumors claiming it will be replaced or upgraded (Disney remains closemouthed on the matter).

### Indiana Jones Epic Stunt Spectacular
**Frommer's Rating:** A+
**Recommended Ages:** 6–adult

Visitors get a peek into the world of movie stunts in this dramatic 30-minute show, which re-creates major scenes from the Indiana Jones series. The show opens on an elaborate Mayan temple backdrop. Indy crashes onto the set via a rope, and, as he searches with a torch for the golden idol, he encounters booby traps, fire, and steam. Then a boulder straight out of *Raiders of the Lost Ark* chases him! The set is dismantled to reveal a colorful Cairo marketplace where a sword fight ensues, and the action includes virtuoso bullwhip maneuvers, gunfire, and a truck bursting into flames. An explosive finale takes place in a desert scenario. Throughout this, guests get to see how elaborate stunts are pulled off. Arrive early and sit near the stage if you want a shot at being picked as an audience participant. Alas, it's a job for adults only. Younger kids may prefer a seat a bit farther away from all the action, and I've found that the mid- to upper rows offer the best views.

### Jim Henson's Muppet*Vision 3-D
**Frommer's Rating:** A+
**Recommended Ages:** All ages

This must-see film stars Kermit and Miss Piggy in a delightful marriage of Jim Henson's puppets and Disney audio-animatronics, special-effects wizardry, 70mm film, and cutting-edge 3-D technology. The coming-right-at-you action includes flying Muppets, cream pies, and cannonballs, plus high winds, fiber-optic fireworks, bubble showers, even an actual spray of water. Kermit is the host; Miss Piggy sings "Dream a Little Dream of Me"; Statler and Waldorf critique the action (which includes numerous mishaps and disasters) from a balcony; and Nicki Napoleon and his Emperor Penguins (a full Muppet orchestra) provide music from the pit. In the preshow area, guests view an entertaining Muppet video on overhead monitors. Note the cute Muppet fountain out front and the Muppet version of a Rousseau painting inside. The 25-minute show (including the 12-min. video preshow) runs continuously.

*Tip:* Sweetums, the giant but friendly Muppet monster, usually interacts with a few kids sitting in the front rows during the show. If you want to sit up front, move to the leftmost theater door in the preshow area.

### Lights, Motors, Action! Extreme Stunt Show
**Frommer's Rating:** B+
**Recommended Ages:** 5–adult
This stunt show features high-flying high-speed movie stunts full of pyrotechnic effects and more. Like the **Indiana Jones Stunt Spectacular** (p. 164), the storyline has the audience following the filming of an action-packed movie (in this case, a spy thriller set in a Mediterranean village). More than 40 vehicles are used in the show including cars, motorcycles, and watercraft—each modified to perform the rather spectacular stunts. It's entertaining and certainly offers its share of thrills, but it's not as engaging as the Indiana Jones production unless you're a car buff. Although the outdoor stadium seating is set back from the action, the noise level is extremely high—and completely unavoidable, no matter where you sit. Very young children may find it overwhelming. Check the entertainment schedule for show times.

**Frommer's Rating:** B

**Recommended Ages:** 8–adult

Once hosted by the late Walter Cronkite and Robin Williams, the current version of **Magic of Disney Animation** features Mushu, the dragon from Disney's *Mulan,* as he co-hosts a theater presentation where some of Disney's animation secrets are revealed. The Q&A session that follows allows guests to ask questions about the animation process before attempting their own Disney character drawings while under the supervision of a working animator (a big hit with adults—don't miss it!). Currently joining in on the fun for a meet-and-greet opportunity are the stars of *Up*—even Mickey makes an occasional appearance; keep in mind, however, that the lineup has changed several times in the past few years and will likely change again.

### Playhouse Disney—Live on Stage!

**Frommer's Rating:** B

**Recommended Ages:** 2–5

Younger audiences love this 20-minute show where they meet characters from the Little Einsteins, Mickey Mouse Clubhouse, Handy Manny, and other popular preschool-favorites. The show encourages preschoolers to dance, sing, and play along with the cast. The action happens several times a day. Check your show schedule.

### Rock 'n' Roller Coaster (Moments)

**Frommer's Rating:** A+

**Recommended Ages:** 10–adult

This inverted roller coaster is one the best and definitely the hippest thrill rides at WDW. It's a fast-and-furious indoor ride in semidarkness. You sit in a 24-passenger "stretch limo" outfitted with 120 speakers that blare Aerosmith at 32,000 watts! Flashing lights deliver a variety of messages and warnings, including "prepare to merge as you've never merged before." Then, faster than you can scream "I want to live!" (around 2.8 sec., actually), you shoot from 0 to 60 mph and into the first gut-tightening inversion at 5Gs. It's a real launch followed by a wild ride through a make-believe California freeway system. One of three inversions cuts

hype says, it's similar to sitting atop an F-14 Tomcat. (I've never
been in an F-14, so I can't argue.) The smooth ride lasts 3 minutes,
12 seconds, the running time of Aerosmith's hit, "Sweet Emotion."
*Note:* Riders must be at least 48 inches tall, and expectant moms
and people prone to motion sickness or those with heart, neck, or
back problems shouldn't try to tackle this ride.

## Sounds Dangerous Starring Drew Carey

**Frommer's Rating:** C

**Recommended Ages:** 8–Adult

Drew Carey provides laughs while dual audio technology provides
some hair-raising effects during this 12-minute show at ABC
Sound Studios. You'll feel like you're right in the middle of the
action of a TV pilot featuring undercover police work and plenty
of mishaps. Even when the picture disappears and the theater is

---

> ### (Tips) Buzz & Woody Are Back in Action
>
> **Toy Story Mania** ★★★ made its debut in 2008. This inter-
> active attraction, based on the popular Disney/Pixar *Toy
> Story* movies, featuring several classic midway-style games,
> each with a *Toy Story*—and technological—twist. Shrunk to
> the size of a toy and sporting 3-D glasses, guests attempt
> to score points at the various booths that line the midway.
> Similar to **Buzz Lightyear's Space Ranger Spin** at the
> Magic Kingdom (p. 131), onboard cannons will fire at the
> targets as characters, including Buzz, Bo Peep, Woody, and
> even the little green men, cheer everyone on as they play.
> Hidden targets will earn you extra points and lead to differ-
> ent levels of play, ensuring that each experience will be dif-
> ferent than the last. *Note:* If you've got little ones (or even
> if you don't), be sure everyone hits the restrooms before
> getting in line here.

plunged into darkness (an effect that will likely turn off younger audience members), you continue on Detective Charlie Foster's chase via headphones that show off "3-D" sound effects.

*Tip:* After the show is over, check out **Sound Works,** which offers interactive activities that allow you to experiment with different sound effects.

## Star Tours

**Frommer's Rating:** B+

**Recommended Ages:** 8–adult

Cutting-edge when it opened, **Star Tours,** based on the original *Star Wars* trilogy (George Lucas collaborated on the ride), is now a couple of rungs below the latest technology but is still fun. The preshow has R2-D2 and C-3PO running an intergalactic travel agency (it offers some of the best detailing of any preshow at Disney World). After boarding a 40-seat "spacecraft," you're off with a whoosh on a journey that takes you through some of the more famous scenes from the movies, full of sudden drops, crashes, and oncoming laser blasts as you seemingly career out of control. *Note:* Riders must be at least 40 inches tall. Also, expectant mothers and people with neck, back, and heart problems or those prone to motion sickness shouldn't ride. There are, however, plenty of places to focus your vision other than the screen (unlike some of the newer simulator rides) if you begin to feel a bit green. *Note:* At press time, Disney had announced plans to completely overhaul the Star Tours experience, bringing with it all-new immersive elements, 3-D effects, and familiar scenes from the entire *Star Wars* saga. The project is slated for completion in 2011 (though an exact date has yet to be set).

## The Twilight Zone Tower of Terror (Moments)

**Frommer's Rating:** A+

**Recommended Ages:** 10–adult

This is a truly stomach-lifting (and dropping) ride, and Disney continues to fine-tune it to make it even better. The legend says that during a violent storm on Halloween night 1939, lightning struck the Hollywood Tower Hotel, causing an entire wing and an elevator full of people to disappear. And you're about to meet them

*Zone.* Eerie corridors lead to a dimly lit library, where you can hear a storm raging outside. After various spooky adventures, the ride ends in a dramatic climax: a 13-story free-fall in stages. The ride features random drop sequences, allowing for a real sense of the unknown (and a different experience every time you ride), and visual, audio, and olfactory effects make the experience even more frightening. Some believe this rivals (even exceeds) Rock 'n' Roller Coaster in the thrill department (one of the Imagineers who designed the tower admitted that he's too scared to ride his own creation). At 199 feet, it's the tallest ride in WDW. ***Note:*** You must be at least 40 inches tall to ride, and expectant moms and people prone to motion sickness or those with heart, neck, or back problems shouldn't try to tackle it. Your stomach may need a few minutes to find its way back to where it belongs after it's all over.

### Voyage of the Little Mermaid
**Frommer's Rating:** B+
**Recommended Ages:** 4–adult
Hazy lighting creates an underwater effect in a reef-walled theater and helps set the mood for this charming musical based on the Disney feature film. The show combines live performers with more than 100 puppets, movie clips, and innovative special effects. Sebastian sings the movie's Academy Award–winning song, "Under the Sea"; the ethereal Ariel shares her dream of becoming human in a live performance of "Part of Your World"; and the evil Ursula, 12 feet tall and 10 feet wide, belts out "Poor Unfortunate Soul." It has a happy ending, as most of the young audience knows it will; they've seen the movie. This 17-minute show is a great place to rest your feet on a hot day, and you get misted inside the theater to further cool you off.

## PARADES, PLAYGROUNDS & MORE
**Disney's Block Party Bash**, the Studio's big parade, made its debut in 2008, replacing Disney Stars and Motor Cars. Guests are invited to sing and dance along as fan-favorites from Disney-Pixar flicks such as *Finding Nemo, Toy Story 2, Monster's, Inc., The*

*Incredibles,* and *A Bug's Life* (among others) take to the streets in this new interactive dance party parade.

**One Man's Dream** is an exhibit on Mickey Ave. A self-guided tour lets you explore the inspirations behind the chapters in Disney's life as well as memorabilia and artifacts from the creative empire he set in motion. ***Note:*** At press time, the exhibit was closed for refurbishment.

Aside from the parades, there are character-greeting hot spots at the **Animation Courtyard,** on the north end of the **Streets of America,** at **Pixar Place** near Toy Story Mania, at the **Magic of Disney Imagination,** at the **Sorcerer's Hat,** and at **Journey into Narnia: Prince Caspian.** See the handout *Times Guide* for the schedule.

## SHOPPING AT DISNEY'S HOLLYWOOD STUDIOS

With more than 20 shops in the park, we can't list them all, but some of the Studios' more unique offerings include:

The **Animation Courtyard Shops** carry collectible cels, costumes from Disney classic films, and pins.

**Sid Cahuenga's One-of-a-Kind** sells autographed photos of the stars, original movie posters, and star-touched items such as canceled checks signed by Judy Garland and others.

**Celebrity 5 & 10,** modeled after a 1940s Woolworth's, has movie-related merchandise: *Gone With the Wind* memorabilia, Hollywood Studios T-shirts, movie posters, Elvis mugs, and more.

---

# 6 ANIMAL KINGDOM

---

Disney's fourth major park opened in 1998 and combines exotic animals, the elaborate landscapes of Asia and Africa, and the prehistoric lands of the dinosaur. Animals, architecture, and lush surroundings take center stage here, with a handful of rides thrown in for good measure.

A conservation venue as much as an attraction, Animal Kingdom ensures that you won't find the animals blatantly displayed throughout the 500-acre park; instead, naturalistic habitats blend seamlessly into the spectacular surroundings. This unfortunately means that, at times, you'll have to search a bit to find the inhabitants. Expect your experience here to be quite different from that at Disney's other parks. It's the spectacular surroundings, meticulously re-created architecture, and intricate detailing, not so much the attractions sprinkled throughout (even though **Expedition Everest** is pretty impressive), that make the park so unique and so interesting. First bonus: Because this is one of Disney's less ride-intensive parks, it's easily enjoyed in a single day, usually less, making it a good choice when you need to cut back and take it a bit slower and easier. Second bonus: The best shows in all of Disney can be found here; **Finding Nemo–The Musical** and the **Festival of the Lion King** should definitely be on your to-do list.

Animal Kingdom is divided into the **Oasis,** a shopping area near the entrance that offers limited animal viewing; **Discovery Island,** home of the Tree of Life, the park's very unique icon; **Camp Minnie-Mickey,** the Animal Kingdom equivalent of Mickey's Toontown Fair in the Magic Kingdom but without any of the fun little rides; **Africa,** where you can wander the village streets and head out on safari (you'll find the largest concentration of animals here); **Asia,** with Mt. Everest looming on the horizon (within it, the coolest thrill ride in the park), includes a raging river ride, exotic animal exhibits (including Bengal tigers and giant fruit bats), and a bird show; and **DinoLand U.S.A.,** filled with carnival-style rides and games, a large play area, and a herky-jerky thrill ride that transports you back in time.

Most of the rides are accessible to guests with disabilities, but the hilly terrain, large crowds, narrow passages, and long hikes can make for a strenuous day if there's a wheelchair-bound person in your party. Anyone with neck or back problems, as well as pregnant women, may not be able to enjoy rides such as **Expedition Everest, Kali River Rapids,** and **Dinosaur.**

The 145-foot-tall **Tree of Life** is in the center of the park. It's an intricately carved free-form representation of animals, handcrafted by a team of artists over the period of a year. The impressive tree has 8,000 limbs, 103,000 leaves, and 325 mammals, reptiles, bugs, birds, dinosaurs, and Mickeys in its trunk, limbs, and roots. For more on the tree, see "Discovery Island," below.

**ARRIVING**    From the parking lot, walk or (where available) ride one of the trams to the entrance. Also, make certain to note where you parked (section and row). Lot signs aren't as prominent as in the Magic Kingdom, and the rows look alike when you come back out. Upon entering the park, consult the handout guide map for special events or entertainment. If you have questions, ask park staffers.

## SERVICES & FACILITIES IN ANIMAL KINGDOM

**ATMS**    Animal Kingdom has an ATM near Garden Gate Gifts to the right of the entrance as well as in DinoLand across from the Primeval Whirl.

**BABY CARE**    The Baby Care Center is located near Creature Comforts gift shop on the west side of the Tree of Life. You can buy disposable diapers at Guest Relations.

**CAMERAS & FILM**    You can drop film off for same-day developing at the Kodak Kiosk in Africa and Garden Gate Gifts near the park entrances. Cameras and film are available in Disney Outfitters in Safari Village; at the Kodak Kiosk in Africa, near the entrance to the Kilimanjaro Safari; and in Garden Gate Gifts.

**FIRST AID**    The First Aid Center, which is staffed by registered nurses, is located near Creature Comforts gift shop on the west side of the Tree of Life.

**LOCKERS**    Lockers ($7–$9, plus a $5 refundable deposit) are located in Garden Gate Gifts to your right as you enter the park. They're also located to the left, near Rainforest Cafe.

**Tips** **Animal Kingdom Tip Sheet**

1. Arrive at opening or stay until near closing for the best view of the animals.
2. **Expedition Everest** offers the biggest thrills in the park, and a FASTPASS may be your only ticket to avoiding the ride's excruciatingly long lines.
3. **Kilimanjaro Safaris** is one of the most popular rides and the best place to see a lot of animals in one sitting. But in summer, the animals can be scarce during the midday heat. If you can hoof it there first thing, do it. If not, try late in the day. The same applies to viewing the gorillas on the **Pangani Forest Exploration Trail.**
4. **Finding Nemo–The Musical** and the **Festival of the Lion King** shows are a must.
5. Looking for Disney characters? Go to the Character Greeting Trails in **Camp Minnie-Mickey.**
6. Make Advanced Reservations for a meal at **Yak & Yeti,** the parks newest themed full-service restaurant.

**LOST CHILDREN**   A center for lost children is located near Creature Comforts at the Baby Care Center on the west side of the Tree of Life. This is also the site of same-day lost and found. At the risk of repeating myself, *make your younger kids wear name-tags inside their clothing.*

**PET CARE**   Pet facilities are located just outside the park entrance ($13–$23 per day; ✆ **407/824-6568**). There are four other kennels located in the WDW complex. (See chapter 2 for more information.) Proof of vaccinations is required.

**STROLLERS**   Stroller rentals are available at Garden Gate Gifts to the right as you enter the park ($15 for a single, $31 for a double, length-of-stay rentals are available at $13 per day for a single, $27 per day for a double—payment in full is expected at time of rental). There are also satellite locations throughout the park. Ask a Disney employee to steer you.

**WHEELCHAIR RENTAL**   You can rent wheelchairs at Garden Gate Gifts to the right as you enter the park. Rentals are $12 for a standard wheelchair; $50 for an electric wheelchair (plus a $20 refundable deposit). Ask Disney employees for other rental locations throughout the park.

## THE OASIS

This painstakingly designed landscape of streams, grottoes, and miniwaterfalls sets the tone for the rest of the park. This is a good place to see wallabies, tiny deer, giant anteaters, sloths, iguanas, tree kangaroos, otters, and macaws). But the thick cover provides a camouflage for the animals and sometimes makes seeing them difficult. There are no rides in this area, and, aside from the animals, it's mainly a pass-through zone.

## DISCOVERY ISLAND

Like Cinderella Castle in the Magic Kingdom and Spaceship Earth in Epcot, the 14-story **Tree of Life** located here has been designed to be the park's central landmark. The man-made tree and its carved animals are the work of Disney artists. Teams of them worked for 1 year creating the various sculptures, and it's worth a stroll on the walks around its roots, but most folks are smart to save it for the end of the day. (Much of it can be seen while you're in line for **It's Tough to Be a Bug!** or on the **Discovery Island Trails**.) The intricate design makes it seem as if a different animal appears from every angle.

### Discovery Island Trails
**Frommer's Rating:** B
**Recommended Ages:** All ages
The old, pre-FASTPASS queue for It's Tough to Be a Bug! provides a leisurely path through the root system of the Tree of Life and a

chance to see real, not-so-rare critters, such as axis deer, red kanga-roos, otters, flamingos, lemurs, Galápagos tortoises, ducks, storks, and cockatoos. Again, the best viewing times are early or late in the day.

### It's Tough to Be a Bug!

**Frommer's Rating:** A, C for young ones scared silly from sensory effects

**Recommended Ages:** 5–adult

This show's cuteness quotient is enough to earn it a B+. But it goes a rung higher thanks to the preshow: To get to the theater, you have to wind around the Tree of Life's 50-foot base, giving you a front-row look at this man-made marvel. After you've passed that, grab your 3-D glasses and settle into a sometimes creepy-crawly seat. Based on the film *A Bug's Life,* the special effects in this mul-timedia show are pretty impressive. It's not a good one for very young kids (it's dark and loud) or bug haters, but for others it's a fun, sometimes poignant look at life from a smaller perspective. Flick, Hopper, and the rest of the cast—ants, beetles, spiders, and, ugh, a stink bug—awaken your senses with, literally, some in-your-face action. And the show's finale always leaves the crowd buzzing.

## DINOLAND U.S.A.

Enter by passing under Olden Gate Bridge, a 40-foot Brachiosau-rus reassembled from excavated fossils. Speaking of which, until late summer 1999, this land had three paleontologists working on the very real skeleton of Sue, a monstrously big *Tyrannosaurus rex* unearthed 9 years earlier in the Black Hills of South Dakota. They patched and assembled the bones here because Disney helped pay for the work. Alas, Sue's permanent home is at Chicago's Field Museum, but DinoLand U.S.A. has a replica cast from her 67-mil-lion-year-old bones. It's marked as **Dino-Sue** on park guide maps.

### The Boneyard

**Frommer's Rating:** B+ for children, B for parents who need to rest their feet

**Recommended Ages:** 3–12

Kids love the chance to slip, slither, slide, and slink through this giant playground and dig site where they can discover the real-looking remains of triceratops, *T. rex,* and other vanished giants. Contained within a latticework of metal bars and netting, this area is popular, but not as inviting as the *Honey, I Shrunk the Kids* play area in Disney's Hollywood Studios.

### Dinosaur
**Frommer's Rating:** B
**Recommended Ages:** 8–adult

This ride hurls you through the darkness in CTX Rover "time machines" back to the time when dinosaurs ruled the earth. The expedition takes you past an array of snarling and particularly ferocious looking dinosaurs, one of whom decides you would make a great munchie. What started out as a journey back through time becomes a race to escape the jaws of an irritated and rather ugly Carnotaurus. Young children may find the large lizards and the darkness a bit frightening, while everyone will find the ride a bit jarring. ***Note:*** You must be 40 inches or taller to climb aboard. Also, expectant mothers and people with neck, back, and heart problems or those prone to motion sickness shouldn't ride.

### Finding Nemo—The Musical
**Frommer's Rating:** A+
**Recommended Ages:** All ages

Disney's new, live stage production is simply enchanting. Nemo, Marlin, Dory, Crush, and Bruce (among other film favorites) come to life before your eyes. Live actors, in creatively designed puppet-like costumes, work together to re-create the undersea adventure made popular by the hit Disney/Pixar film *Finding Nemo.* Stunning special effects (making this one of the best and most unique stage productions in all of Disney) and a moving musical score (written especially for the show by the composers of the Tony award–winning *Avenue Q*) complete the experience. Even with a slight tweak in the storyline, you'll find yourself thoroughly engrossed from start to finish thanks to the absolutely entrancing

performances that, at times, spill into the entire theater. It's a must
see for the entire family.

### Primeval Whirl

**Frommer's Rating:** B+

**Recommended Ages:** 8–adult

Disney introduced this spinning, free-style twin roller coaster in 2002 in an effort to broaden the park's appeal to young kids (odd, as this ride has a pretty tall height minimum). You control the action through its wacky maze of curves, peaks, and dippity-do-dahs, encountering faux asteroids and hokey cutouts of dinosaurs. This is a cross between those old carnival coasters of the '50s and '60s and an expanded version of the **Barnstormer** at Goofy's Wise-acre Farm (p. 128). *Note:* The ride carries a 48-inch height mini-mum, and expectant moms as well as those with neck, back, or heart problems and folks prone to motion sickness should stay planted on firm ground.

### TriceraTop Spin

**Frommer's Rating:** B+ for tykes and parents

**Recommended Ages:** 2–7

Cut from the same cloth as the Magic Carpets of Aladdin at WDW's Magic Kingdom, this is another minithrill for youngsters. In this case, the cars look like cartoon dinosaurs. They circle the hub while gently moving up and down and all around.

## CAMP MINNIE-MICKEY

Disney characters are the main attraction in this land designed in the same vein as an Adirondack resort. Aside from those characters, however, this zone for the younger set isn't nearly as kid-friendly as rival Mickey's Toontown Fair in the Magic Kingdom (reviewed earlier in this chapter).

### Character Greeting Trails (Moments)

**Frommer's Rating:** A for kids, D for waiting parents

**Recommended Ages:** 2–12

Some say this is a must-do for people traveling with children; I say run the other way—quickly. If, however, your kids are hooked on getting every character autograph possible, this is the place to go. A variety of Disney characters, from Winnie the Pooh and Pocahontas to Timon and Baloo, have separate trails where you can meet and mingle, snap photos, and get those autographs. Mickey, Minnie, Goofy, and Pluto even make periodic appearances. Be aware, however, that the lines for these meet-and-greet opportunities are at times excruciatingly long, so unless your kids are really gung ho on collecting the characters' signatures, don't even think of coming here. *Note:* Disney introduced a new character experience in 2009—each and every evening at closing time (near the park exit), Mickey, Minnie, and Goofy wave good night to their guests as they head back to their hotels for the night.

### Festival of the Lion King (Finds)
**Frommer's Rating:** A+
**Recommended Ages:** All ages

Almost everyone in the audience comes alive when the music starts in this rousing 28-minute show in the Lion King Theater. It's one of the top three theme-park shows in Central Florida. The production celebrates nature's diversity with a talented, colorfully attired cast of singers, dancers, and life-size critters leading the way to an inspiring sing-along that gets the entire audience caught up in the fun. Based loosely on the animated film, this stage show blends the pageantry of a parade with a tribal celebration. The action is on stage as well as moving around the audience. Even though the pavilion has 1,000 seats, it's best to arrive at least 20 minutes early.

## AFRICA

Enter through the town of Harambe, a worn and weathered African coastal village poised on the edge of the 21st century. (It actually took a great deal of effort to create the run-down appearance.) The whitewashed structures, built of coral stone and thatched with reed by African craftspeople, surround a central marketplace rich with local wares and colors.

### Kilimanjaro Safaris
**Frommer's Rating:** A+ early or late, B+ other times
**Recommended Ages:** All ages

Animal Kingdom doesn't have many rides, but the animals you'll see on this one make it a winner as long as your timing is right. They're scarce at midday during most times of year (cooler months being the exception), so I recommend you ride it as close to park opening or closing as possible. If you don't make it in time for one of the first or last journeys, the lines can be horrific, so a FAST-PASS is almost a must.

A large rugged truck takes you through the African landscape (though just a few years ago it was a cow pasture). The animals usually seen along the way include giraffes, black rhinos, hippos, antelopes, Nile crocodiles, zebras, wildebeests, cheetahs, and a pair of lions that may offer half-hearted roars toward some gazelles that are safely out of reach. Early on, a shifting bridge gives riders a brief thrill; later, you get a bit of drama (a la Disney) as you help catch some poachers. While everyone has a good view, photographers may get a few more shots when sitting on the left side of their row.

### Pangani Forest Exploration Trail (Finds)
**Frommer's Rating:** B+, A if you're lucky enough to see the gorillas
**Recommended Ages:** All ages

The hippos put on quite a display (and draw a riotous crowd reaction) when they do what comes naturally and use their tails to scatter water over everything above and below the surface. There are other animals here, including ever-active mole rats, but the **lowland gorillas** are the main event. The trail has two gorilla-viewing areas: One sports a family, including a 500-pound silverback, his ladies, and his children; the other has bachelors. Guests who are unaware of the treasures that lie herein often skip or rush through it, missing a chance to see some magnificent creatures. That said, they're not always cooperative, especially in hot weather, when they spend most of the day in shady areas out of view. There's also an Endangered Animal Rehabilitation Centre with colobus and mona monkeys.

### Rafiki's Planet Watch (Overrated)
**Frommer's Rating:** C
**Recommended Ages:** All ages

Board an open-sided train (the Wildlife Express) near Pangani Forest Exploration Trail for a trip to the back edge of the park, which has three attractions. **Conservation Station** offers a behind-the-scenes look at how Disney cares for animals (the entrance mural is loaded with Hidden Mickeys). You'll pass nurseries and veterinarian stations. But these facilities need to be staffed to be interesting, and that's not always the case. Older kids and adults will find the audio presentations at the sound booths pretty neat. **Habitat Habit!** is a trail with small animals such as cotton-top tamarins. The **Affection Section**'s petting zoo has rare goats and potbelly pigs, but not much more.

## ASIA

Disney's Imagineers have outdone themselves in creating the kingdom of **Anandapur.** The intricately painted artwork and detailed carvings are very appealing, and they even seem to make the lines move a tad faster.

### Expedition Everest
**Frommer's Rating:** A+
**Recommended Ages:** 8–adult
**Expedition Everest** is Animal Kingdom's first true thrill ride. Your journey begins in the small Himalayan village of Serka Zong, where guests board the Anadapur Rail Service for a seemingly casual trek to the snowcapped peak of Mount Everest. Upon departing, you'll pass through an Asian mountain range and dense bamboo forests, and then move past glacier fields and pounding waterfalls. But your journey will quickly get off track (almost literally) and become an out-of-control high-speed train ride that sends you careening along rough and rugged terrain, moving backward and forward along icy mountain ledges and through darkened caves—only to end up confronting the legendary Yeti. Bet your adrenaline is running already. The meticulous and painstaking detail is some of the most impressive in all of WDW. Prayer flags are strung between the aged and distressed buildings, while intricately carved totems, stone carvings, and some 2,000 authentic handcrafted Asian objects are scattered throughout the village.

### Flights of Wonder

**Frommer's Rating:** C+

**Recommended Ages:** All ages

This live-animal action show has undergone several transformations since the park opened. It's still a low-key break from the madness and has a few laughs, including Groucho the African yellow-nape, who entertains the audience with his op-*parrot*-ic a cappella solos. For thrills there's the just-above-your-head soaring of a Harris hawk and a Eurasian eagle owl. To entertain guests waiting in line for the show, trainers will often bring out an owl or hawk, allowing for an up-close look and the opportunity to learn some interesting facts about the stars of the show.

### Kali River Rapids

**Frommer's Rating:** B+

**Recommended Ages:** 6–adult

Its churning water mimics real rapids, and the ride's optical illusions will have you wondering if you're about to go over churning falls. The ride begins with a peaceful tour of lush foliage, but soon you're dipping and dripping as your tiny craft is tossed and turned. The snowcapped peak of Expedition Everest makes a brief but impressive appearance along the way. If the rapids themselves don't drench you, the kids manning water cannons along the route will ensure you get wet—sometimes even soaked—hence the cart selling oversize towels and socks just beyond the ride's exit. (Bring a plastic bag for your valuables. The rafts' center storage areas alone likely won't keep them dry.) The lines can be long, but keep your head up and enjoy the marvelous art overhead and on beautiful murals. *Note:* There's a 38-inch height minimum, and expectant moms and people with neck, back, and heart problems or those prone to motion sickness shouldn't ride it.

### Maharajah Jungle Trek

**Frommer's Rating:** B

**Recommended Ages:** 6–adult

Disney keeps its promise to provide up-close views of animals with this exhibit. If you don't show up in the midday heat, you may see

Bengal tigers through a wall of thick glass, while nothing but air separates you from dozens of giant fruit bats hanging in what appears to be a courtyard. Some have wingspans of 6 feet. (If you have a phobia, you can bypass this, though the bats are harmless.) Guides are on hand to answer questions, and you can also check a brochure that lists the animals you may spot; it's available on your right as you enter. You'll be asked to "recycle" it as you exit.

## PARADES

**Mickey's Jammin' Jungle Parade** is an interactive street party featuring whimsical colorful animals and characters on expedition. The music and overall atmosphere are lively and the one-of-a-kind visuals are some of the best in all the parks.

# 7 DISNEY WATER PARKS

## TYPHOON LAGOON

Located off Buena Vista Drive between the Downtown Disney Marketplace and Disney's Hollywood Studios, **Typhoon Lagoon** ★★★ is the ultimate in themed water parks. Its fantasy setting is a palm-fringed island village of ramshackle, tin-roofed structures, strewn with cargo, surfboards, and other marine wreckage left by the "great typhoon." A storm-stranded fishing boat (the *Miss Tilly*) dangles precariously atop 95-foot Mount Mayday, the steep setting for several attractions. Every half-hour, the boat's smokestack erupts, shooting a 50-foot geyser of water into the air.

### Essentials

In summer, arrive no later than 9am to avoid long lines. The park is often filled to capacity by 10am and then closed to later arrivals. Beach towels ($2.50 per towel) and lockers ($8 and $10) can be rented, and beachwear can be purchased at **Singapore Sal's.** There are picnic tables (consider bringing picnic fare; you can keep it in your locker until lunch). Guests aren't permitted to bring their own flotation devices, and glass bottles are prohibited.

Hop onto a raft or an inner tube and meander along **Castaway Creek,** a 2,100-foot lazy river that circles most of the park. It tumbles through a misty rainforest, then by caves and secluded grottoes, while passing meticulously maintained tropical foliage. Tubes are included in the admission price.

The newest thrill to splash onto the scene is **Crush 'n' Gusher,** a first-of-its-kind water coaster featuring three separate experiences to choose from. **The Banana Blaster, Coconut Crusher,** and **Pineapple Plunger** each offer steep drops, twists, and turns of varying degrees as you're sent careening through an old, rusted-out fruit factory. Intense jets of water actually propel riders back uphill at one point.

Many of the park's other attractions require guests to be older children, teens, or adults, but **Ketchakiddie Creek** is a **kiddie area** exclusively for 2- to 5-year-olds. An innovative water playground, it has bubbling fountains to frolic in, mini–water slides, a pint-size "white-water" tubing run, spouting whales and squirting seals, rubbery crocodiles to climb on, grottoes to explore, and waterfalls to loll under. It's also small enough for you to take good home videos or photographs.

Guests are given free equipment (and instruction) for a 15-minute swim through **Shark Reef,** a very small snorkeling area that includes a simulated coral reef populated by about 4,000 parrotfish, angelfish, yellowtail damselfish, and other cuties including small rays and sharks. If you don't want to get in, you can observe the fish via portholes in a walk-through viewing area.

The **Typhoon Lagoon Surf Pool** is a large (2.75-million gal.) and lovely lagoon, the size of two football fields and surrounded by a white sandy beach. It's the park's main swimming area. The chlorinated water has a turquoise hue much like the Caribbean. **Large waves** roll through the deeper areas every 90 seconds. A foghorn sounds to warn you when one is coming. Young children can wade in the lagoon's more peaceful tidal pools—**Blustery Bay** or **Whitecap Cove.** The lagoon is also home to a **special weekly surfing program.**

## (Tips) Water Park Do's & Don'ts

1. Go in the afternoons, about 2pm, even in summer, if you can stand the heat that long and want to avoid crowds. The early birds usually are gone by then.

2. Go early in the week when most of the weeklong guests are filling the lines at the theme parks.

3. Kids can get lost just as easily at a water park as at the other parks, and the consequences can be tragic. All Disney parks have lifeguards, usually wearing bright red suits, but, to be safe, make sure *you* are the first line of safety for the kids in your crew.

4. Women should remember the one-piece bathing suit rule I mentioned above under "Water Slides." And all bathers should remember **the "wedgie" rule** on the more extreme rides, such as Summit Plummet (at Blizzard Beach, below). What's the "wedgie" rule? It's a principle of physics that causes you to start out wearing baggies and end up in a thong.

5. Use a waterproof sunscreen with an SPF of at least 30 and drink plenty of fluids. Despite all that water, it's easy to get dehydrated in summer.

**Humunga Kowabunga** consists of three 214-foot Mount May-day slides that propel you down the mountain on a serpentine route through waterfalls and bat caves and past nautical wreckage before depositing you into a bubbling catch pool; each offers slightly different views and 30-mph thrills. There's seating for non-Kowabunga folks whose kids have commissioned them to "watch me." Women should wear a one-piece swimsuit on the slides (except those who don't mind putting on a show for gawkers). *Note:* You must be 48 inches or taller to ride this. **Storm Slides** offer a tamer course through the park's man-made caves.

**Mount Mayday** is the setting for three white-water rafting adventures—**Keelhaul Falls, Mayday Falls,** and **Gangplank Falls**— all offering steep drops coursing through caves and passing lush scenery. Keelhaul Falls has the most winding route, Mayday Falls has the steepest drops and fastest water, and the slightly tamer Gangplank Falls uses large tubes so that the whole family can pile on.

## BLIZZARD BEACH

**Blizzard Beach** ★★★ is the younger of Disney's water parks, a 66-acre "ski resort" in the midst of a tropical lagoon centering on the 90-foot, uh-oh, Mount Gushmore. Apparently a freak snowstorm dumped tons of snow on Walt Disney World, leading to the creation of Florida's first—and, so far, only—mountain ski resort (complete with Ice Gator, the park's mascot). Naturally, when temperatures returned to their normal broiling range, the snow bunnies prepared to close up shop, when they realized—this is Disney, happy endings are a must—that what remained of their snow resort could be turned into a water park featuring the fastest and tallest waterlogged "ski" runs in the country. The park is located off World Drive, just north of the All-Star Movie, Music, and Sports resorts.

### Essentials

Arrive at or before opening to avoid long lines and to be sure you get in. Beach towels ($2.50 per towel) and lockers ($8 and $10) are available.

### Major Attractions in the Park

Inner-tubers can float lazily along the park-circling, 2,900-foot **Cross Country Creek,** but beware of the mysterious Polar Caves where you'll get splashed with melting ice. **Melt-Away Bay** is a 1-acre bobbing wave pool fed by waterfalls of melting "snow" and features relatively calm waves. **Runoff Rapids** is another tube ride, though this one lets you careen down any of three twisting-turning runs, one of which sends you through darkness.

Designed for tweens and teens, **Ski-Patrol Training Camp** features a rope swing, a T-bar drop over water, slides like the wet and slippery **Mogul Mania** from the Mount, and a challenging ice-floe walk along slippery floating icebergs. The **Slush Gusher** super-speed slide travels along a snow-banked gully. *Note:* It has a 48-inch height minimum. The three flumes of the **Snow Stormers** descend from the top of Mount Gushmore and follow a switch-back course through ski-type slalom gates.

Before thinking about **Summit Plummet,** read *every* speed, motion, vertical-dip, wedgie, and hold-onto-your-breast-plate warn-ing in this guide. Then, test your bravado in a bullring, a space shuttle, or dozens of other death-defying hobbies as a warm-up. This puppy starts pretty slowly, with a lift ride to the 120-foot summit. Then . . . well . . . kiss any kids or religious medal you may be car-rying. Because, if you board, you *will enter* the self-proclaimed world's fastest body slide (I believe it!), a test of your courage and swimsuit that virtually goes straight down and has you moving *sans* vehicle at 60 mph by the catch pool (aka, stop zone). Even the hardiest rider may find this one hard to handle; a veteran thrill-seeker described the experience as "15 seconds of paralyzing fear." *Note:* It has a 48-inch height minimum. Also, expectant mothers and people with neck, back, and heart problems shouldn't ride.

**Teamboat Springs** is the World's longest white-water raft ride, where your six-passenger raft twists down a 1,200-foot series of rushing waterfalls. **Tike's Peak** is a kid-size version of Mount Gushmore offers short water slides, rideable animals, a snow castle, a squirting ice pond, and a fountain play area for young guests.

**Toboggan Racers** is an eight-lane slide that sends you racing head first over exhilarating dips into a "snowy slope."

# 8  OTHER WDW ATTRACTIONS

## FANTASIA GARDENS & WINTER SUMMERLAND

**Fantasia Gardens Miniature Golf** ★★, located off Buena Vista Drive across from Disney's Hollywood Studios, offers two 18-hole miniature courses drawing inspiration from the Walt Disney classic cartoon of the same name. You'll find hippos, ostriches, and alligators on the **Fantasia Gardens** course, where the Sorcerer's Apprentice presides over the final hole. Seasoned minigolfers probably will prefer **Fantasia Fairways,** which is a scaled-down golf course complete with sand traps, water hazards, tricky putting greens, and holes ranging from 40 to 75 feet.

Santa Claus and his elves provide the theme for **Winter Summerland** ★★, which has two 18-hole miniature golf courses across from Blizzard Beach on Buena Vista Drive. The **Winter** course takes you from an ice castle to a snowman to the North Pole. The **Summer** course is pure Florida, from sandcastles to surfboards to a visit with Santa on the "Winternet."

Tickets at both venues are $12.52 for adults and $10.39 for children 3 to 9. Both are open from 10am to 10 or 11pm daily. For information about Fantasia Gardens, call ✆ **407/560-4582.** For information about Winter Summerland, call ✆ **407/560-3000.** You can find both on the Internet at **www.disneyworld.com**.

## ESPN WIDE WORLD OF SPORTS COMPLEX

The 200-acre ESPN Wide World of Sports Complex (known until 2009 as Disney's Wide World of Sports) has a 7,500-seat professional baseball stadium, 10 other baseball and softball fields, six basketball courts, 12 lighted tennis courts, a track-and-field complex, a golf driving range, and six sand volleyball courts. It's a haven for sports fans and wannabe athletes.

The complex is located on Victory Way, just north of U.S. 192 (west of I-4; ✆ **407/939-1500;** www.disneyworldsports.com). It's open daily from 10am to 5pm; the cost is $12.61 adults, $9.34 kids 3 to 9. Organized programs and events include:

- The **Multi-Sports Experience** challenges guests with a variety of activities, covering many sports: football, baseball, basketball, hockey, soccer, and volleyball. It's open only on select days.

- The **Atlanta Braves** play 16 spring-training games during a 1-month season that begins in early March. Tickets cost $15 to $28. For tickets call Ticketmaster (© **407/939-4263**).
- The **NFL, NBA, NCAA, PGA,** and **Harlem Globetrotters** also host events, sometimes annually and sometimes more frequently, at the complex. Admission varies by event.

# 7

# Fast Facts

## 1 FAST FACTS: ORLANDO

**AMERICAN EXPRESS**   There's an American Express Travel Service Office located at 7618 W. Sand Lake Rd. (© **407/264-0104**).

**BABYSITTERS**   Many Orlando hotels, including all of Disney's resorts, offer in-room babysitting services, usually from an outside service such as **Kid's Nite Out** (© **800/696-8105** or 407/828-0920; www.kidsniteout.com) or **All About Kids** (© **800/728-6506** or 407/812-9300; www.all-about-kids.com). Rates for in-room sitters usually run $14 to $16 per hour for the first child and another $2 to $3 per hour for each additional child. A premium fee of $2 per hour (not per child) is often added for services provided during unusually early or late hours. A transportation fee of approximately $10 to $12 is usually charged as well.

**DOCTORS & DENTISTS**   There are basic first-aid centers in all of the theme parks. There's also a 24-hour, toll-free number for the **Poison Control Center** (© **800/282-3171**). To find a dentist, call the **Dental Referral Service** at © **800/235-4111** or go online to **www.dentalreferral.com**.

   **Doctors on Call Service** (© **407/399-3627**) makes house and room calls in most of the Orlando area (including the Disney resorts). **Centra Care** has several walk-in clinics listed in the Yellow Pages, including ones on Sand Lake Road, near Universal (© **407/851-6478**); at Lake Buena Vista, near Disney (© **407/934-2273**); and on U.S. 192 (W. Irlo Bronson Hwy.) in the Formosa Gardens shopping center (© **407/397-7032**). Another good source for medical care in the Orlando area is the **Medical Concierge,** a division of the

EastCoast Medical Network (© **407/648-5252;** www.themedical
concierge.com), makes "hotel house calls," has a walk-in clinic
(listed in the Yellow Pages), arranges emergency dental appoint-
ments, and rents medical equipment.

**DRINKING LAWS**   The legal age for purchase and consumption
of alcoholic beverages is 21; proof of age is required and often
requested at bars, nightclubs, and restaurants, so it's always a good
idea to bring ID when you go out. No liquor is served in the Magic
Kingdom at Walt Disney World. Alcoholic drinks are available,
however, at the other Disney parks. Do not carry open containers
of alcohol in your car or any public area that isn't zoned for alcohol
consumption. The police can fine you on the spot.

**EMERGENCIES**   Call © **911** to report a fire, contact the police,
or get an ambulance.

The Florida Tourism Industry Marketing Corporation, the state
tourism promotions board, sponsors a **help line** (© **800/647-9284**).
With operators speaking more than 100 languages, it can provide
general directions and can help with lost travel papers and credit
cards, minor medical emergencies, accidents, money transfer, airline confirmation, and much more.

**HOSPITALS**   Emergency room care is available at **The Florida
Hospital** (© **407/764-4000**), located at 400 Celebration Place in
Celebration, just minutes south or the main U.S. 192 tourist area).
**Dr. P. Phillips Hospital** (formerly the Sand Lake Hospital), 9400
Turkey Lake Rd. (© **407/351-8500**), is about 2 miles south of
Sand Lake Road. From the WDW area, take I-4 east to the Sand
Lake Road exit and make a left on Turkey Lake Road. The hospital
is 2 miles up on your right. To avoid the highway, take Palm Parkway (off of Apopka–Vineland near Hotel Plaza Blvd.); it turns into
Turkey Lake Road. The hospital is 2 miles up on your left. **Celebration Health** (© **407/303-4000**), located in the near-Disney
town of Celebration, is at 400 Celebration Place. From I-4, take
the U.S. 192 exit. At the first traffic light, turn right onto Celebration Avenue. At the first stop sign, take another right. *Note:* Be
sure to check with your healthcare provider or insurance carrier
regarding regulations for medical care outside your home area.

**LOST CHILDREN**    Every theme park has a designated spot for adults to be reunited with lost children (or lost spouses—it happens). Ask where it is when you enter any park (or consult the free park guide maps), and instruct your children to ask park personnel (not a stranger) to take them there if they get separated from you. Point out what park personnel look like so they will know whom to go to. Children age 7 and younger should wear name-tags inside their clothing (if you're carrying a cellphone, put the number on the tag).

**MAPS**    Maps of the Orlando area can be found online at **www. visitflorida.com** and **www.orlandoinfo.com**, as well as at the official visitor center and at most area hotels. Maps of the Disney theme parks, Universal theme parks, and SeaWorld parks can be found on their respective websites, as well as at the theme parks themselves.

**NEWSPAPERS & MAGAZINES**    The *Orlando Sentinel* is the major local newspaper, but you can also purchase the Sunday editions of other papers (most notably, the *New York Times*) in some hotel gift shops or bookstores such as Barnes & Noble or Borders. Don't count on finding daily editions of West Coast papers, such as the *Los Angeles Times,* without making special arrangements. The Friday edition of the *Sentinel* includes extensive entertainment and dining listings, as does the *Sentinel*'s website, **www.orlandosentinel. com**. *Orlando Weekly* is a free, alternative paper that has a lot of entertainment and art listings focused on events outside tourist areas.

**POLICE**    Call ✆ **911** in an emergency.

**POST OFFICE**    The post office most convenient to Disney is at 10450 Turkey Lake Rd. (✆ **800/275-8777**). It's open Monday through Friday from 9am to 7pm, Saturday from 9am to 5pm. A smaller location, closer to Disney, is at 8536 Palm Pkwy., in Lake Buena Vista, just up the road from Hotel Plaza Boulevard (✆ **800/ 275-8777**). If all you need is to buy stamps and mail letters, you can do that at most hotels.

**SMOKING**   If you're a smoker, light up where and when you can. Smoking is prohibited in many of Florida's public places. All Disney resorts are now nonsmoking, and though you're still permitted to inhale in most outdoor areas, the Disney parks restrict where. *Note:* Don't expect to light up during dinner. In 2002, Florida voters approved a constitutional amendment that bans smoking in public workplaces, including restaurants and bars that serve food. Stand-alone bars that serve virtually no food and designated smoking rooms in hotels are exempt.

**TAXES**   A 6% to 7.5% sales tax (depends on the local county you happen to be in) is charged on all goods with the exception of most edible grocery-store items and medicines. Hotels add another 3% to 6% in resort taxes to your bill, so the total tax on accommodations can run you up to 13.5%.

**TIME**   Orlando is in the **Eastern Standard Time (EST)** zone, which is 1 hour later than Chicago, 3 hours later than Los Angeles, 5 hours earlier than London, and 12 hours earlier than Sydney.

**TIPPING**   In hotels, tip **bellhops** at least $1 per bag ($2–$3 if you have a lot of luggage) and tip the **chamber staff** $1 to $2 per day (more if you've left a disaster area for him or her to clean up). Tip the **doorman** or **concierge** only if he or she has provided you with some specific service (for example, calling a cab for you or obtaining difficult-to-get theater tickets). Tip the **valet-parking attendant** $1 every time you get your car.

In restaurants, bars, and nightclubs, tip **service staff** and **bartenders** 15% to 20% of the check, tip **checkroom attendants** $1 per garment, and tip **valet-parking attendants** $1 per vehicle.

As for other service personnel, tip **cab drivers** 15% of the fare; tip **skycaps** at airports at least $1 per bag ($2–$3 if you have a lot of luggage); and tip **hairdressers** and **barbers** 15% to 20%.

# INDEX

See also Accommodations and Restaurant indexes, below.

## ACCOMMODATIONS